Forgive for Love

Forgive
for
Love

The Missing Ingredient for a

Healthy and Lasting Relationship

———◆———

Dr. Fred Luskin

HarperOne
An Imprint of HarperCollinsPublishers

HarperOne

FORGIVE FOR LOVE: *The Missing Ingredient for a Healthy and Lasting Relationship.* Copyright © 2007 by Dr. Fred Luskin. All rights reserved. Printed in the United States of America. No part of this book may be used or reproduced in any manner whatsoever without written permission except in the case of brief quotations embodied in critical articles and reviews. For information address HarperCollins Publishers, 10 East 53rd Street, New York, NY 10022.

HarperCollins books may be purchased for educational, business, or sales promotional use. For information please write: Special Markets Department, HarperCollins Publishers, 10 East 53rd Street, New York, NY 10022.

HarperCollins Web site: http://www.harpercollins.com
HarperCollins®, 🏭®, and HarperOne™ are
trademarks of HarperCollins Publishers.

FIRST HARPERCOLLINS PAPERBACK EDITION PUBLISHED IN 2009

Designed by Joseph Rutt

Library of Congress Cataloging-in-Publication Data is available upon request.

ISBN 978-0-06-123495-8

09 10 11 12 13 RRD(H) 10 9 8 7 6 5 4 3 2 1

Contents

ONE

The Missing Factor

Dana and Greg came to see me soon after they ran into serious relationship problems. Their love for and commitment to each other was apparent, but it was also clear that the past was eating away at the present. When Dana and Greg first met, he was still dealing with the emotional turmoil of his recent divorce. Greg clung to Dana like a drowning person clings to a life preserver. Dana's previous relationship and subsequent divorce had occurred a few years earlier, and she, though needy, was no longer in crisis. During our time together, I helped Greg forgive his first wife, Gloria, so that he was better able to see Dana as a new and distinct person. And I helped Dana to understand Greg's neediness and also to forgive herself for choosing a partner who was in the middle of a difficult time in his life.

Dana also realized that she had work to do to forgive Greg for his insecurity and the difficulties that caused. Learning how to forgive helped to prevent Greg's and Dana's pasts from damaging their present. Forgiveness saved their relationship and gave them skills to understand that letting go of grudges and resentment would be a critical part of maintaining a loving and lasting relationship.

Greg and Dana are just one example of a couple for whom forgiveness has been essential for navigating the challenges that all relationships face. Relationship issues may emerge when partners are at different developmental stages, or when they have different needs and expectations—for example, when one partner wants children and the other does not, or when one partner wants to move for a job and the other does not. Many couples struggle with caretaking for aged parents or with being overwhelmed by work. In our busy and hectic lives, it is difficult for many of us to find the energy and time to deal successfully even with life's normal struggles.

Luke was in his forties when he met thirtysomething Diane. He already had two kids from a first marriage, and she wanted two of their own. Luke loved and wanted Diane, but did not want more children. Diane wanted more children, and she also wanted Luke. They were both convinced that the other was insensitive because both heard only the other's rejection of their own needs. It took a lot of work, but eventually forgiveness allowed Luke and Diane to talk to each other and lovingly accept the limitations of entering a relationship with a person with different life desires and goals.

From relative interest in sex to dedication to work to relationships with parents and children, there are simply too many ways in which a relationship can become unbalanced. Considering how complex life can be, it is inevitable that we will disagree with our partners on things both important and not so important. The key is to understand the inevitability of disagreement and the need to forgive the inevitable and to move on with love. In this book, you will learn how to do this, and you will also see for yourself the immediate value of forgiveness in your relationship when you discover that it is an essential balm for hurt feelings.

Committed relationships are hard work, and they ask a lot of us. According to the triangle theory of romance, it takes passion, friendship, and commitment to sustain a relationship. Relationships falter when they have two of these elements but lack the third. If you both love and like your partner but aren't committed, your relationship will end eventually. If you feel friendship with and commitment to your partner, you'll end up with a good friend, not a lover. If you have commitment and passion without friendship, you will end up with a stormy but passionate mess. In order for your relationship to work, you need to love your partner, like your partner, and be willing to stick it out through thick and thin.

As director of the Stanford University Forgiveness Project, I have probably taught more people to forgive in the United States than anyone else during the past decade. I have conducted the largest successful forgiveness research study to date, and my research has proven that forgiveness heals a wide range of emotional and psychological issues—from severe trauma such as the murder of a child to dealing with the loss of money in the stock market. I have taught forgiveness in corporate settings, in medical and law schools, at numerous churches and synagogues, and in a host of other religious and secular settings. Also, I have trained numerous therapists in my forgiveness methods and helped them learn to use my work in their practices.

In addition, I have worked with thousands of disappointed and angry couples and individuals who have been hurt in their relationships. Listening to countless stories of infidelity, alcohol abuse, mistreatment of children, disregard for feelings, and other causes of divorce and disagreement, I have seen firsthand how difficult it is to make relationships work. In fact, my dozen years of teaching and research on forgiveness have convinced me of just how hard it is to have a loving and lasting union. But more than that, this work has shown me how essential forgiveness is and why it needs to be at the center of our relationships.

Forgive for Love shows how to forgive the things people do to the ones they love. The skills taught in this book not only will help you come to terms with a grievance or disagreement in the past, but will also enable you to prevent problems from developing in your current relationship, no matter how good it is.

The tools discussed in this book are for people in a committed relationship. I often use the word "marriage," but you do not need to be married to find these tools beneficial. They will also work in your relationship with a significant other, a life partner, or a lover. The book is primarily for people who have chosen a life partner or have been dating one person for an extended period of time and want their relationship to work. The principles can also be applied to other long-term relationships in which disagreement is inevitable, such as those with your parents, your children, or your longtime friends. However, even though most of the ideas in *Forgive for Love* can help you in any relationship, the book is not designed as a guide to casual dating.

Think about it. The centrality of commitment in relationships is expressed through the marriage vows, which ask us to love our partners through richer and poorer, in sickness and in health, and for better and for worse until death. That means that we promise to love them when they are not doing well, when they have failed, when life is not exactly turning out as hoped, or when we're going through a financial reversal. What I see in the marriage vows is a basic prescription: if we want our relationships to last, we better be prepared to forgive. The vows make it clear that over the life of a marriage we will experience difficulty and pain and that it is our responsibility to stay connected to our partners. How could we possibly do this without forgiveness? What other form of healing would clean the slate and give us fresh eyes and an open heart?

Unfortunately, most examinations of successful relationships have neglected the subject of forgiveness. Until now, forgiveness has not been front and center as an aid to a sustainable marriage. *Forgive for Love* is the first book to explore forgiveness from both a scientific and a clinical perspective.

My entire professional career has led me to believe that forgiveness is central to a happy and functional relationship. I am licensed as a therapist to work with individuals, couples, and children and have earned two advanced degrees from prestigious universities. I have been supervised by excellent clinicians and first-rate therapists. About fifteen years ago, I got a master's degree in psychology and a license as a marriage and family counselor. Following that, I received a doctorate and a license as a clinical psychologist after numerous classes, much training, six thousand hours of clinical supervision, and a two-part licensing examination.

In all these years of study and experience, I was never once taught the importance of forgiveness in helping two people become a successful couple. Forgiveness was not one of the interventions I learned, nor was it a topic for supervision and clinical training. When I began the Stanford Forgiveness Project, there were only a handful of published studies that showed the positive effects of teaching people to forgive. My education and training left a void in my ability to help couples that I had to fill myself.

Hundreds of self-help books are available to guide couples as they navigate the changing phases of a marriage. There are books that teach couples how to improve their communication by learning to really talk and listen to each other. There are books that teach couples how to have better sex and books about managing conflict. Many of these volumes are helpful, and I have used a number of them myself to teach classes. Yet finding advice about how to practice forgiveness is like looking for the oyster with the pearl hidden in it. There are good books out there on enriching your marriage, but they almost always lack explicit advice about the importance of forgiveness and specific steps for practicing forgiveness.

Too many of us simply don't know how valuable forgiveness is in a relationship, let alone how to forgive. Communicating better, improving our conflict resolution skills, and learning to have better sex are all great for our relationships. The problem is that even if we get better at all of these aspects of a relationship, we still disagree and occasionally mistreat each other. Forgiveness will always be necessary, because couples always have significant personality differences and conflicts with each other.

Forgive for Love is the first book that teaches you how to enfold forgiveness into the heart of your relationship. In this book, I show you that forgiveness is the missing piece in the difficult puzzle of creating a successful marriage.

John Gottman of the Gottman Institute, which focuses on re-searching and restoring relationships, conducted a scientific study of why some marriages succeed and others fail by interviewing and tracking hundreds of couples through the University of Washington. Before Gottman's work, we could only guess as to why some couples had successful marriages and others did not. He turned the study of marriage into a science. One of his most provocative findings was that approximately 70 percent of the issues that couples disagree about at the beginning of their rela-tionship do not change over time.

What this means, for instance, is that if you have a stronger libido than your partner when you are dating, there is a good chance that you will still be more libidinous after fourteen years together. If you are a person who craves order and your partner is a mess, neither of you will have changed after three years of being together. If you are more adventuresome than your partner early in the relationship, you are likely to be the one to suggest the exotic vacation on your fifteenth anniversary. Without forgiveness, these personality differences can turn into grudges between you and your partner that over time will erode the relationship.

I wrote *Forgive for Love* to be the essential missing link in the literature on successful relationships. *Forgive for Love* shows you how to use forgiveness to communicate better, manage conflict better, see the good in your partner, and allow yourself to make common mistakes. It shows you the critical importance of forgiving yourself, the value of modeling forgiveness for your children, and step-by-step instruction in how to do this.

People who learn to forgive have more successful relationships. Successful couples are able to figure out how to forgive each other for being themselves, and they do this because they know that it is nearly impossible to change other people. Since we are human beings, by definition we are imperfect. Unsuccessful couples do not learn how to forgive each other. They live with grudges that separate them until the relationship slowly disintegrates or quickly blows up. Successful couples learn how to make peace with the fact that they are both human beings with flaws, quirks, and annoying habits. Unsuccessful couples spend angry years in futile attempts to change each other and then fan the smoldering resentment that emerges.

The cost of bad marriages in the United States is staggering. Over 50 percent of marriages end in divorce. Forty-three percent of all first marriages end within the first ten years, and 60 percent of second and third marriages end in the first ten years. Thus, people who do not succeed at marriage the first time around are likely to be even less successful the second or third time around. These remarkable statistics show how hard it is to create a good relationship that lasts. One survey showed that only 25 percent of spouses consider themselves "happy together." Somewhere around 50 percent of children are raised by one parent at some point in their lives, and many of these children are being raised in poverty. Obviously there is a lot of room for improvement in how we conduct our marriages and relationships.

If couples only had to forgive each other for their differences, or for being flawed but human, that would be hard enough. Some of our flaws and human failings can be really annoying. Our partners may be guilty of sloppiness, chronic lateness, laziness, self-absorption, grumpiness, dressing badly, eating in a hurry, and so on. Relationship problems can be aggravated by differing natural rhythms, such as bedtimes and wake-up times, levels of physical activity, and frequency of sex. Couples can also be strained by issues associated with the relative importance of money, neatness, and the effort each partner puts into the relationship. And partners often bring different views of what's "normal" to parenting, family relationships, politics, good grades, and other aspects of life.

The quest for forgiveness is even harder, however, when marriage partners bring bigger problems to the relationship than personality differences and individual quirks. Spouses may cheat, lie, have long-term affairs, steal money or possessions, or live in a fantasy world of their own creation. Others spend too much money on frivolous things or refuse to have sex. Some spouses abuse alcohol and drugs, are bad parents, or are indifferent to their partners. Whether they are selfish and mean or scared and lonely, such spouses can be difficult to deal with.

Over the course of almost any relationship, some problems will be caused by personality differences and some problems will be caused by selfish and mean behavior. It is in your best interest to learn to forgive all the obstacles that are thrown your way in your primary relationship, whatever their source. To do this you must give yourself time to feel your pain and to process what transpired so that you can make a good decision as to what to do next. When forgiveness is on your menu, you can do this with a more open heart and a clearer mind.

Partners in any complex human relationship will often need to forgive themselves and each other. *Forgive for Love* shows you how to forgive your partner, both for being human and for being unkind. Here you will learn how to make peace with the person you chose and how to repair the damage when you are treated badly. The book fills a critical gap in our knowledge about how to make relationships last, and it will help you find peace and happiness with your partner and with yourself. Forgiveness is a fundamental and critical component of a healthy relationship. Turn the page and let's learn why and how to use it.

Forgive for Love Quiz

Please answer yes or no to the following questions.

1. Are there some things about your partner that regularly bug you? Yes No

2. Do you find yourself verbally expressing frustration with your partner even when they aren't present? Yes No

3. Have you made a promise to yourself to talk calmly with your partner and then found yourself talking more harshly than you intended? Yes No

4. When you are hurt by your partner do you talk more about what is wrong with them than about your hurt feelings? Yes No

5. When you think about something your partner did that upsets you does it remind you of other things they have done wrong? Yes No

6. Do you often feel that your partner just doesn't get it when you try to talk to them? Yes No

7. Do you find that time after time it is the same issues that continue to upset you about your partner? Yes No

8. Do you long for someone who does not have your partner's faults? Yes No

9. When you argue with your partner do you bring up their wrongs from the past? Yes No

10. When you talk about your relationship with other people is your partner often the villain? Yes No

11. Do you get annoyed at your partner because they do not listen well? Yes No

12. Do you often think that if only your partner would change, your relationship would be better? Yes No

The key:

If you answered yes to:

0–2: You are doing a good job of keeping resentment at bay and can successfully manage the normal disagreements of a relationship. You need this book only if you are in a new relationship to prepare for issues that have yet to surface. Or you need this book if you are going through a particularly good patch but have had some issues in the past. There is no bad time to learn the skills of forgiveness.

3–5: It is critical that you start practicing forgiveness right away. Most likely, you are aware of your relationship strengths and your problems are manageable. However, bitterness is emerging and without forgiveness as part of your recipe of responses long term damage can be done to your relationship.

6–12: Your relationship is in trouble. Either you are going through a really bad patch or you struggle with chronic negativity. Regardless, your relationship needs help. Learning to forgive is necessary to make sure the damage done to your relationship is contained and further damage is not done. The healing of the relationship can start with this book and lasting and loving relationship can still be yours.

◆

TWO

What Is Forgiveness and Why Is It Good for Me?

Everybody thinks they know what it is to forgive, but the truth is that many people are unclear about what forgiveness actually is. They form their understanding of forgiveness from old church sermons or from snippets of information in magazines or movies. Couples often do not choose forgiveness when it would be helpful to their relationship because their understanding of forgiveness is so limited. Once a couple understands what it means to forgive and give it a try with each other, they quickly see a positive effect in their relationship. A big part of my work is simply explaining what forgiveness is and showing couples the benefits of learning how to forgive. Too many couples remain stuck in contempt and negativity and miss out on a terrific way to improve their relationship simply because they don't understand this basic tool.

How can you forgive your partner if you do not know what forgiveness is? How can you learn to forgive if no one has ever shown you how? Both of these questions came up when I was working in couple's therapy with Billy and Kathy. Billy was a Vietnam vet who had struggled with alcohol abuse since his service days. Kathy never drank, had worked hard as a school-teacher, and had diligently protected their children from the effects of Billy's drinking. When I saw them, their children were grown and they were trying to figure out how to make a life together with an empty nest. At our first appointment, I learned that Billy had stopped drinking about two years earlier, for health reasons. His doctor had bluntly told him that if he continued to drink he was a dead man.

Kathy was furious with Billy for his years of alcohol abuse, and for the first three sessions she angrily described to me how awful their life had been during his drinking years. She filled the room with complaints about his parenting and his irresponsible behavior. Billy apologized for his poor behavior, but his belated regret was not enough for Kathy. Billy wasn't a bad man; he was one of the thousands of men who returned from the Vietnam War with emotional problems so bad that it took alcohol to numb them. Like many vets, he never learned coping mechanisms to help him deal with the horrendous experiences he'd had in Vietnam. When he wasn't drinking, Billy was a good-natured and well-liked man who kept a job no matter how bad he felt. There was affection in the marriage: Kathy saw her husband's good points, and he thought the world of her. However, when I asked her, "What will it take for you to forgive him?" her response was, "Never. What he did was unforgivable."

Kathy explained that what she found unforgivable was that Billy had drunk to the point of being drunk with kids in the house. She believed that if she forgave Billy now, she would be saying that his drinking had been okay, when clearly it wasn't. Before Kathy could begin the process of forgiving Billy and healing her marriage, she needed to understand what forgiveness was and what it would mean to forgive her husband. After we started talking about the nature of forgiveness, she was finally able to let go of some of her resentment so that she and Billy could discuss their current relationship and help it get back on track.

I have seen hundreds of patients like Kathy who are in relationships in which they have been hurt or misunderstood. They suffer from emotional pain so intense, and have had life-altering experiences so profound, that they can't let go of their grudges. But because they misunderstand what it means to forgive, they are unable to use its healing power in their relationships.

If you are in a relationship that needs healing, the first thing you need to understand is what forgiveness is and why common misconceptions of forgiveness get in the way of truly practicing it. I'll discuss case histories of couples who were able to practice real forgiveness, and I'll also show you how forgiveness contrasts with similar qualities, such as reconciliation, condoning, and pardoning.

Forgiveness is not a cure-all. In some situations, forgiveness is not the right choice. If you are in an abusive relationship, it is more important to find safety than to practice forgiveness. If you have been molested and your abuser is still active, then stopping the abuser is more important than forgiving him or her. If you are suffering from a new loss or recent infidelity, it is important to feel the pain and grieve the loss, not simply rush to forgive the offender. Forgiveness is not a substitute for making good decisions that protect you and the ones you love. Forgiveness is not a substitute for feeling hurt and struggling to know what to do. What forgiveness brings is a sense of peace that allows you to make decisions that are unclouded by bitterness or resentment.

What Is Forgiveness?

One of my favorite explanations of forgiveness comes from *The Lion King* in the words of Timon and Pumba, who counsel Simba to "leave your past behind you." We can also think of forgiveness as "giving up all hope for a better past," and at least one part of forgiveness is planning the future rather than lamenting the past. While this idea of turning away from the past is one aspect of forgiveness, it doesn't fully explain the importance of forgiveness and its power to heal wounds. I find that two central components of forgiveness articulate best how this works.

The first element of forgiveness is the ability to be accepting when your spouse fails to give you what you want or imposes on you something you don't want. This aspect of forgiveness helps you to remain at peace when your partner says no to a request or demand that you find reasonable. It also helps you to stay calm when you don't get something you think you deserve. This aspect of forgiveness is utilized every day, such as when you ask your husband to take out the garbage and he doesn't get around to doing it. You might think that it would be better if he had done the chore, but you do not feel angry or violated about it. You can use the same technique when your husband does something you think he shouldn't have.

Let's say that you have to be up early every morning and your wife can sleep late. You ask her to get into bed without disturbing you, and she agrees to do so. Yet, at least twice a week, she wakes you up to have sex or talk or she simply makes noise or a mess. The fact that you are disturbed when you don't want to be becomes a problem in your relationship.

I am going to teach you how to stay calm even when the trash can is still full of garbage or when you are awakened against your wishes. Staying calm does not make you a doormat. In fact, there is great power in knowing that you don't have to be an emotional mess even though the trash didn't get taken out or your need for sleep wasn't respected. The ability to remain at peace when you do not get what you want is forgiveness. Being able to forgive puts you on the path to a strong and successful relationship and life.

Forgiveness reminds you that it is not just what your partner does, or does not do, that causes you pain. Much of your suffering comes from having wanted your partner to do something different from what he or she actually did. You wanted the garbage to be taken out and got garbage staying inside instead. You wanted peace and quiet and got a rude awakening. You wanted a neat house and came home to a mess. When you want something different from what you actually get, you are always in a position of struggle. That struggle often shows up as anger or despair or a sense of helplessness. The good news is that you can get over those negative emotional reactions and learn to be at peace.

For example, you can believe that taking out the garbage is the right thing to do and forgive your husband when he does not do it. You can believe that he should do what you ask, but forgive him for not doing it. You can forgive your husband for resisting your attempts to motivate him, and you can forgive yourself for not finding the key that makes him do what you want. You can want the garbage removed and remain at peace when it is not. The important principle here is that your partner makes the decision to take out the garbage or not. Whether or not you remain at peace is mostly up to you. Forgiveness contains the understanding that another person's action, no matter how awful, does not compel you to be endlessly miserable, angry, or emotionally distraught.

Perhaps you are in the mood for sex, but your partner is not. Maybe you have an arrangement that if one partner wants sex, the other will try to comply. However, it's just not happening tonight. Your lover is in a foul mood and is simply not going to oblige you and has said no to what you want. When you forgive your partner, you are emotionally okay with your partner's refusal to have sex while remaining certain that sex is what you want. You can stay cool, while also being clear that your partner has let you down. The decision not to have sex when you wanted it was your partner's, and it is your decision how much agitation you feel in response. It is up to you how you deal with your partner's decision to say no.

The ability to remain calm, or to regain your calm after being upset, has significant implications for your physical and emotional well-being. *Forgive for Love* will explain that being able to remain calm when your wishes are unfulfilled is an essential skill in a successful marriage. If you are honest with yourself, you will agree that not getting exactly what you want from your partner is a major challenge in even a good relationship. One reason this happens is that we experience such minor disappointments on a regular basis. Our partners do things against our wishes every day, and even if they do what we want sometimes, it is not exactly the way we wanted. Learning how to cope with this successfully is essential.

Suppose that you ask your partner to turn off the outside light before going to sleep. Every night you ask him to turn out the light, but every morning you wake up and the light is on. You ask again the next evening, and once again when you wake up the light is on. Your partner is effectively saying no to your desires by his actions, and it is likely that your response is to feel anger or a sense of not being listened to. However, there is a part of you that can be at peace in this situation. That part of you has already forgiven your partner and is not offended by his behavior. That part hasn't been offended by your partner's choice to ignore your wishes or by not getting what you wanted. Sometimes this forgiveness shows up as a small voice in your head reminding you that you are getting out of control. It may remind you that even though your partner misbehaved today, he made dinner and took the kids all over town yesterday. Helping you to uncover this part of yourself when you need it is the purpose of this book.

The ability to stay calm even when you do not get what you want enables you to be responsible for your moods and thoughts even though your lover has done something you don't like. This ability to forgive will save wear and tear on your nervous system as well as allow you to communicate with your partner without skyrocketing blood pressure or negative emotions. Forgiveness does not require you to stop asking for what you want. Nor does it suggest that there is something wrong with you for wanting your partner to take out the garbage or turn out the lights. Forgiving your partner does not mean you have to accept everything your lover does. It simply means you can contentedly live with your lover without getting upset every time he or she chooses to ignore your wishes.

Of course, when larger issues than the garbage or a lack of sex are at stake, partners *can* hurt each other. Sometimes our partners say no when we are asking them to assume legitimate and important responsibilities. In these situations, the implications of their refusal can be dire. We can learn to be at peace, however, even with a huge no. Donna struggled with her boyfriend Jerry for years because he could not or would not keep a job. Jerry would stick at a job for a while, but lose it when he started showing up late or mouthing off to his boss. Donna and Jerry went through this routine many times during their relationship. Jerry spent his days honing his golf game or playing video games, while Donna worked fifty hours a week at a job that involved a long commute. Needless to say, this situation was difficult for Donna, and at times it drove her crazy

Donna told me she was certain that Jerry was capable of sustained employment. She was convinced that he was a terrible partner because he did not pay his share of the household expenses.

Jerry was giving Donna a big "no" in an important part of their life together, and the situation had become a black-and-white one for her. Jerry did not share in the labor and expenses of maintaining a home, and he continued to resist Donna's efforts to get him to contribute. He did not keep jobs long enough to become a partner in this area of the relationship. When I first saw Donna, she was far from peace or forgiveness ... in fact, she was livid. But when she learned about forgiveness, she was able to ease Jerry out of her home and be at peace. She also forgave herself for putting up with such an unequal contribution for such a long time.

The second central component of forgiveness is the passage of time between offense and forgiveness. For instance, do you have to come to peace immediately when your husband totals the car? Do you have to be calm when your wife is snorting the rent money up her nose? When offenses are this serious, the answer is no, but with minor offenses the answer should be yes. You can be at peace very quickly with how the garbage and the lights are handled, but it takes time when the issue is as important as infidelity or abandonment. Although such losses, injustices, or offenses are other ways of not getting what you want, dealing with them involves going through a grief process. I believe that forgiveness is the optimal resolution of the grief process. Forgiveness needs to follow any situation in which your hopes have been disappointed.

Couples mistreat each other through a lack of love, dishonesty, and a lack of responsibility. When your lover rejects your desire for sex, you are not getting the love you desired. When your wife lies to you, you are not getting the truth you wanted. When your lover does not change the oil in the car and the engine is fouled, you are not getting the responsibility you wanted. These are common experiences and only a few of the ways in which partners hurt each other. In each situation, part of the natural reaction is grief.

Grief is a biological reaction to a serious loss such as the death of a spouse or child. It works as a protective mechanism to help us cope with loss and to give us time and space to regain trust. As we grieve, forgiveness helps to change the loss from an open wound to a healed one. When we are hurt or have suffered a loss, part of our normal response is to grieve the loss. We grieve when our parents die, or when our marriage ends. When a loved one lies to us, we grieve the loss of trust in the relationship. A job loss or career downturn can also cause us to grieve. There are many smaller annoyances that can also cause us pain, such as when our lover does not listen to our account of the day's events.

When you grieve, you feel a combination of anger, sadness, fear, despair, and anxiety. Dwelling on painful thoughts about the loss or betrayal is another part of grief, as are the difficult reflections on the state of your relationship. So, if your spouse is caught cheating with a friend of yours, it is normal and natural to react with pain and outrage. There will be a period of time when you are upset and mistrustful and will certainly question your marriage. Even if the marriage survives, it will be damaged and you will have to work to recommit to it.

If you decide to stay married to your cheating spouse, you will have to acknowledge your pain and bring it into the open. You will grieve the loss of a faithful marriage and the dreams you had about your life together. It will be a struggle to trust your partner again, and the process of doing so will take some time. If you want the marriage to endure, however, your grief has to end at some point. You will need to move on from the negative emotions and turmoil of the grief stage and start living the rest of your life. This is the point where forgiveness comes into play. Forgiveness is the natural next step after you have articulated the wrong done to you and felt the pain that was inflicted on you.

Forgiveness can wrap up the grief, but it does not prevent the inevitable and necessary suffering. When there is a serious injury or loss, there is no way to avoid pain. If you want to have a satisfactory future, you will need to feel the loss and then let go of the hurt it has caused you. You need to forgive.

Even if you decide to divorce after a betrayal, you will still need to forgive. Interestingly, forgiveness comes into play whether you decide to end the relationship or remain with your partner. This is because both are legitimate responses to the situation. You can forgive with either decision. Let's say you decide to end the marriage. After experiencing much emotional and psychological suffering, you have evaluated your marriage, found it wanting, and decided that you are better off without your spouse. You have to grieve the loss of the marriage, the loss of your dreams of fidelity, and the severing of your trust, all because of your spouse's infidelity. Nevertheless, you will eventually have to replace your grief with something else in order to move on. Forgiveness is the optimal replacement. When you forgive, you are able to be at peace even though rejection, disloyalty, and dishonesty have been a part of your life.

Your best chance for successful future relationships and overall happiness is to forgive your former partner. Forgiveness is not a substitute for grief, nor does it preclude the pain caused by your partner's cheating. But it does gently allow your grief to ebb so that you can move on and live a successful life.

Forgiveness is a lubricant that can restore the health of your relationship whether you remain in it or not. When you combine the two components of forgiveness—staying calm and taking the time to grieve your losses—you are able to return to peace after your lover did not provide you with what you wanted. Forgiveness also allows you to take responsibility for managing your own emotional and psychological responses and to take the time to feel your pain and sort out your thinking.

Forgiveness can benefit you whether or not you stay with your lover because forgiveness is possible even when you are certain that your lover did something wrong. You can forgive even when you have been grievously hurt or when you have suffered for a long time. Forgiveness is an inside job: it has a direct bearing on your ability to cope with your relationship and helps you come to peace so that you can make the best decisions. It will take you awhile to forgive a major wrongdoing, but other things can be forgiven more quickly.

Many couples have common misconceptions about forgiveness that make it harder to put into practice. Some people confuse forgiveness with condoning unkind actions. There are those who think that we forgive in order to repair the relationship with our spouse. Some of us are afraid to forgive because we think that doing so will prevent us from seeking justice. Others believe that forgiveness has to be a precursor to reconciliation, or that forgiveness means forgetting what happened. These ideas are all wrong.

One of the great misconceptions about forgiveness is that it is the same as reconciliation. Reconciliation is deciding whether or not to talk to your lover again after an infidelity. Forgiveness is deciding whether or not to let go of the anger and despair you feel because you did not get the loyal partnership you wanted. Reconciliation means reestablishing a relationship with the person who hurt you. Forgiveness means making peace with a bitter part of your past and no longer blaming your experiences on the offender. You can forgive even if you don't want to have any further relationship with the person who hurt you. In fact, you do this every time you forgive someone who is dead or someone who has left, never to be seen again. Every time you forgive someone you knew for only a short painful moment (like the driver in a hit-and-run accident that killed a loved one) you do this. With forgiveness you have a choice. You can forgive and give the relationship another chance, or you can forgive and move on to a new relationship. The choice is yours.

I am often asked if there is a timetable for how long forgiveness should take. Unfortunately, there are no hard-and-fast guidelines for how forgiveness unfolds. Some people simply grieve longer than others. Some research suggests that the normal grief cycle for major losses is between six months and two years. Sometimes just deciding to forgive can be all we need.

For several weeks Ruth had been angry at Jerry for not attending her sister Joan's wedding. Jerry and Ruth's sister had bickered for years, and when Joan's wedding date came they were not speaking. Ruth took Jerry's snub personally: she was close to Joan, and it hurt her that Jerry had been rude to her sister. One day, though, Ruth realized that her grudge was not helping her relationship, and enough was enough. To Jerry's relief, she let him off the hook. Forgiveness does not mean deciding that what happened to you was okay. Ruth still thought Jerry had been wrong, but she forgave him.

Forgiving someone does not require that you condone that person's unkind, inconsiderate, or selfish behavior. To forgive is to let go of the extra suffering you have imposed on yourself after the normal cycle of grief has run its course. You do not have to be a doormat in order to forgive, nor does being forgiving make it okay for your partner to treat you unkindly. You must know how to say no when your lover crosses a boundary and lies to you. If you have condoned your partner's action, there is no need for forgiveness because you have chosen acceptance instead. We only need to forgive something that we think was the wrong thing to do.

Forgiveness is not the same as forgetting. You should not forget what has happened to you: your life story is important, and there are several important reasons why you want to remember it as it happened. First, remembering allows you to ensure that something bad does not happen again. Josh made a vow to himself that if his new lover Kim drank too much, he was not going to go out with her again. Josh had ignored the early signs of his ex-wife's drinking, and that was why he was cautious with Kim. He had forgiven his first wife, Carol, but also learned a lesson: he now knew that he could not accept excessive drinking in a relationship. Josh did not prejudice his relationship with Kim because of the pain caused by Carol.

Second, remembering what happened allows you to pat yourself on the back for healing and forgiving the things and people that hurt you in the past. You deserve praise for forgiving, letting go, and moving on. You have succeeded on a difficult journey, and that is cause for celebration. You should remember the things that hurt you in order to help yourself heal, not because you feel helpless and victimized by them. Don't go too far: you don't want to dwell on what has happened or get a big head because you have been able to forgive. You do want to acknowledge the perseverance that allowed you to overcome the wounds of your past. You want to feel good about your strength and the decisions you have made.

Third, remembering your past gives you the opportunity to use your healed memories to offer compassion and support to those in need. When you forgive, you are a model for those still struggling. So many people agonize over painful memories and could benefit from the inspirational example of others. When you remember your painful experiences, you are able to offer compassion and support to others. Giving a helping hand to someone who is going through the same experiences you went through can be invaluable to them. Your example demonstrates that forgiveness is possible.

In the same way, to forgive does not mean that we give up claims to justice or compensation. I once worked with a man who was the victim of a hit-and-run accident. Russell was still bitter and in chronic pain nine months after his accident. He insisted that he could not pursue his lawsuit if he forgave the driver. I told him to pursue legal action if that was his choice, but to forgive the driver so that his head would be clear and his decisions sound. The forgiveness was purely for his own emotional and physical well-being. By forgiving the driver, Russell would be a victim of the accident for as little time as possible.

I also knew that the criminal justice system and monetary compensation would not fill Russell's need for emotional healing. Russell needed to win in court as well as in his life; he needed to be successful in his lawsuit and reclaim his heart. I told Russell to set up a two-pronged plan. The first prong was learning to forgive, for his own emotional healing. The second prong was working to ensure that the offender was punished. Russell's two approaches were complementary but not the same. Forgiveness would not ensure a speedy trial, and justice would not necessarily heal Russell's emotional pain.

Susan's ex-husband owed her three years of child support payments. She came to one of my classes and said that she was afraid that if she forgave her ex, she could not pursue him for the money he owed. She thought that forgiving him emotionally meant forgiving his financial obligations. I had to explain to Susan that even if she forgave her ex, she had an ongoing responsibility to protect her children, whether she was furious or at peace. Staying furious at her ex would not help her be a good parent, and neither would allowing him to get away with his payment delinquency.

The most important thing to remember is that forgiveness does not mean giving up your right to be angry when you have been hurt or mistreated. My research shows that when people forgive, they retain their ability to be angry but use that ability more wisely. To forgive is not to condone the hurtful things that our lovers have done to us. In fact, if we condone those actions, we must think that they are okay. If we condone our lovers' past indiscretions, we do not have to forgive them. Forgiveness starts when we think that we have been mistreated and we are hurt and grieving. A wife can choose to condone her husband's lying because he had a bad day. A husband can choose to condone his wife's drinking because she comes from a dysfunctional family. To forgive, on the other hand, is to say that lying is wrong, but we are not going to hold a grudge about it or lose our peace over it. Forgiveness acknowledges that we were disappointed but allows us to not stay stuck in the past.

What Is Forgiveness?

- Forgiveness is for you and not for your partner.

- Forgiveness is taking back your power from being wounded.

- Forgiveness is taking responsibility for how you feel now.

- Forgiveness is about your healing and not about your partner's action.

- Forgiveness is a trainable skill, just like learning to throw a baseball.

- Forgiveness helps you get control over your feelings today.

- Forgiveness can improve your mental and physical health.

- Forgiveness is becoming a hero instead of a victim in the story you tell about what happened.

- Forgiveness is a choice you make.

- Everyone can learn to forgive.

- Forgiveness is about today and not yesterday.

- Forgiveness is making peace when you did not get what you wanted.

- Forgiveness is acknowledging the hurt.

What Forgiveness Is Not

- Forgiveness is not condoning your partner's unkindness.

- Forgiveness is not forgetting that something painful happened.

- Forgiveness is not excusing poor behavior.

- Forgiveness does not have to be an otherworldly or religious experience.

- Forgiveness does not require you to reconcile with your partner.

- Forgiveness does not ask you to give up having painful feelings.

- Forgiveness does not mean you can't take your partner to court to get what is owed you.

- Forgiveness does not mean you have to stay together.

Serena married Bill after they had gone on only a few dates. Most of her friends and family cautioned her to wait, but she knew that Bill was the one. Unfortunately, it took only a few months before Serena found herself alone and with an empty checking account. Notices of overdue bills starting showing up at the same time that Bill began staying out late every night. At the very moment Serena's life started to collapse, she found out she was pregnant. Shortly after that, she learned that almost all of the money from their business was feeding Bill's cocaine and alcohol addictions. When their daughter was born, Bill disappeared for a week. One day he called from another state to say that he would not be home for a while.

This phone call was the worst moment of Serena's life. It got so bad for Serena that her parents had to come and take her to live with them. When Bill eventually returned from his wanderings, he began stalking her and demanding to see his daughter. Serena was scared, vulnerable, and, despite the help of her parents, dependent on welfare.

Slowly, though, she began to rebuild her life. She started graduate school and became a hospital-based nurse. She moved into an apartment with a close friend. In addition, she took a forgiveness class I taught at Stanford University. Through this class Serena let go of her resentment toward Bill and put her time and energy into rebuilding her life and caring for her child.

While reducing her enmity toward Bill may have seemed like a small matter in light of her other problems, Serena felt that learning how to forgive—not forget—Bill for his addiction and abandonment made her next steps possible. She would never forget how bad her life was with Bill drinking and how badly it hurt when Bill left. In our sessions Serena was finally able to say that she thought Bill's abandonment and drug problems were the wrong way for a husband to behave to his wife and child. She was also able to clearly state that she deserved spousal and child support.

Forgiveness allowed Serena to feel less anger. She was still able to get angry, but her anger no longer overwhelmed her. Serena was able to make better choices in her life as her obsession with Bill lessened. She was thinking more about herself and less about him. Serena also found that forgiveness gave her greater appreciation of her child, her parents help, her friends, and her fresh start. When we have less resentment and are able to stop feeling like a victim, it is easier to see the good in our lives. Forgiving Bill helped Serena to see that not reconciling with him was the right decision. She was making her decision based on clarity and decisiveness, not anger or self-pity.

My experience working with thousands of people who have been hurt and who have struggled to forgive has convinced me that the ability to forgive is crucial to health, both emotional and physical. I have seen many people like Serena and Susan who have trouble forgiving their partner for painful experiences. Almost all of them tell me that one of the problems was that they were never shown how to forgive. This lack of knowledge, coupled with misconceptions about forgiveness, explains why so many people do not forgive even the people closest to them.

Before I share the seven steps to forgiveness, I want to explain two other aspects of this process. In chapter 3, I review the research on forgiveness and explain how the mind and body are linked and why forgiving is so good for the health of your mind, body, and relationships. Finally, in chapter 4, I explain the difference between forgiving your partner for a specific offense and becoming a more forgiving marital partner. In the great majority of marriages, it is more important to become a forgiving lover than it is to forgive a specific offense. Learning to be a forgiving lover carries the potential to heal and renew a marriage in which hope has been lost or dreams dashed.

◆

THREE

The Science of Forgiveness

I have been conducting research on the effectiveness of forgiveness for more than ten years. My research shows that learning to forgive improves mental and physical well-being and heals relationships. Although the field is relatively new, there is enough evidence to prove that forgiveness is a positive way to deal with disappointment, loss, and mistreatment. In this chapter, I discuss some amazing research on the effect of forgiveness on physical health. Then I review my research as director of the Stanford Forgiveness Project and show you the research that links forgiveness to successful relationships.

Research shows that learning to forgive or being a forgiving person helps you feel better physically. The reasons are simple. It is very stressful to be constantly at war with certain parts of your life. Telling yourself again and again that you got a raw deal because your husband does not love you the way you want to be loved is hard on your heart and nervous system. Blaming someone who does not care about you enough for the way your life turned out is incredibly stressful. Dwelling on the ex who didn't love you and has since moved on puts a strain on your nervous system and does not slow your ex down at all. Finally, it is stressful and ultimately self-defeating to complain about things you can't change in your spouse. If your wife is messy and has always been messy, constantly expressing your displeasure about it will not do your muscles or arteries any good. Nor will it make you or her feel better or get along any better.

The reality is that resentment and stress can further damage your relationship as well as your nervous system, while forgiveness can reduce the harm caused by these negative feelings. By forgiving, we are able to let go of our resentment and reduce the stress it places on our body. Jan is a good example. She did not appreciate the way her longtime boyfriend yelled at her kids. Whenever she thought about it, she would feel jumpy, her heart rate would rise, and her neck would tighten up. Her feelings of resentment caused her to snap at her kids and feel sorry for herself. When Jan finally learned to forgive her boyfriend, she still tried to get him to change, but she did not hold a grudge against him for his bad behavior. Because she was able to forgive him, Jan's blood pressure went down.

Studies reveal:

- People who are more forgiving report fewer health problems. In addition, learning to forgive may reduce feelings of hostility, a proven risk factor for heart disease.[1]

- People who blame other people for their troubles have a higher incidence of illnesses such as cardiovascular disease and cancer.[2]

- People who harbor resentment and refuse to forgive show negative changes in blood pressure, muscle tension, and immune response.[3]

- People who imagine forgiving their offender note immediate improvement in their cardiovascular, muscular, and nervous systems.[4]

- Angry people with moderately high blood pressure who learn to forgive show a reduction in their blood pressure and their anger.[5]

- A study demonstrates that among people with chronic back pain, those who have forgiven others experience lower levels of pain and fewer associated psychological problems like anger and depression than those who have not forgiven.[6]

- One study of the medical rehabilitation of spinal cord injuries found that patients who are more forgiving of themselves and of others report more life satisfaction.[7]

- The first study connecting forgiveness and health with racially and socioeconomically diverse individuals shows that for low-socioeconomic-status African Americans, forgiveness is linked to low blood pressure and low levels of the stress hormone cortisol.[8]

- People who learn to forgive report less stress and fewer of the physical symptoms of stress.[9]

I have taught forgiveness to people dealing with the pain of everything from the murder of a child to the loss of significant amounts of money. My first forgiveness study served as my dissertation for a PhD degree in counseling and health psychology from Stanford University. One of the reasons I was interested in studying forgiveness was because of a painful struggle I'd had in my own life. I figured that if I had such a difficult time with learning to forgive, others must have had problems forgiving as well. For my experiment I wanted to test whether the methods I had developed and used in my own life might work for others.

Before I started my first study, I assumed certain things about forgiveness that were untested at the time but now serve as a cornerstone of my work. My first assumption was that forgiveness is the same process no matter what type or severity of offense it involves. To me, forgiveness is forgiveness, and learning to forgive is difficult enough without having to sort offenses into different categories. I wondered at the time whether this might be one reason people have such a difficult time forgiving.

I am not claiming that all offenses can be forgiven at the same pace. If your wife commits murder, forgiving her is not the same as forgiving her for getting a parking ticket. However, the process of forgiveness is the same regardless of the offense committed. Unlike prior studies, which had used subjects who were all hurt by the same kind of wrong, I recruited volunteers for my first two studies who had been hurt by a wide range of painful situations.

My second assumption was that forgiveness is more about our present life than about our past. The goal of my forgiveness training is to reduce pain and suffering so that people can move on in their lives. In my own situation, I had realized that the heart of what I was feeling was an inability to find love and happiness in my current life. I blamed the person who hurt me in the past for my unhappiness, but in fact I was upset at the condition of my life in the present. I saw that if I wanted to get better, I would have to focus more on the present and future than on the past.

My third assumption was that the power of forgiveness is wasted when applied only to the worst aspects of people's lives. Why turn to forgiveness only in response to the actions of an abusive lover or an alcoholic spouse? Why not learn to forgive the daily hassles and problems we all face in our relationships? I saw that forgiving smaller offenses would be good practice for forgiving bigger difficulties.

Since I was a graduate student at the time, I decided to conduct my research with the most available population—other students. I recruited student volunteers between the ages of eighteen and thirty who still carried a grudge toward someone close to them or still felt hurt. I worked with students who needed to forgive their parents for hurting them, forgive their teachers for unfair grading, or forgive their close friends for sleeping with their lovers. Some needed to forgive their lovers for cheating on them, forgive their bosses for lying to them, or forgive their sisters or brothers for being the family favorite. I recruited fifty-five volunteers and randomly assigned them to two groups: one that got my forgiveness training immediately and one that received the forgiveness training when the first group was finished.

The second group served as a comparison group to the first group, the so-called forgiveness group. The comparison group demonstrated that positive changes were due to my forgiveness training and not to the passage of time or simply the act of signing up to be in the study. To make sure the groups were truly random I put all of the volunteers' names in a pile and then had a research assistant use a numerical formula to divide them into the two groups. Randomizing the subjects gave me the best chance of having two equal groups to compare. By doing this, I would know that it was my training creating more forgiveness, not that the forgiveness group was naturally more forgiving.

The results of my first study were very positive and validated my hypotheses, with almost all of the positive results being statistically significant. What this means is that the forgiveness group's scores weren't just better than the comparison group's scores, but better for reasons that had little or nothing to do with luck. In experiments of this type, it will often be the case that one group ends up with better scores than the other, but this difference by itself is not enough to ensure that the experiment worked.

Statistical calculations tell you whether the difference is significant and also ensure that your results are not caused by luck or by huge changes made by just one or two subjects. When a result is statistically significant, that means there is a 95 percent certainty that it is not the result of chance.

Each student had to volunteer for my study. The participants also had to complete three written psychological tests: one as they entered the study, the second at the end of the forgiveness training, and the third ten weeks after the training ended. We accepted into the study only students whose scores on the initial test fell in the average or normal range, proving that however much trouble they were having in forgiving someone for a specific issue, they were psychologically and emotionally normal, not depressed or hostile. In fact, on some measures the students were less angry, and wanted less revenge on the offender, than the average person their age.

In scientific research, it is possible to get significantly positive results with people who begin the study in the average range. The goal of almost all psychological research is to get people who start out depressed, anxious, or angry to end the experiment close to the average range. My students started at average and still improved significantly. My results showed me that almost everyone can benefit from learning to forgive.

My experiment was conducted with a group of college students who had been hurt and were stuck in their pain. The students did not know how to release their hurt and move on. My experiment showed that learning to forgive helped them improve their psychological and emotional functioning in a variety of ways. I am proud to say that the positive results of the six hours of forgiveness training remained unchanged two and a half months after the training ended. When the students signed up for the experiment, they did not know whether they would be in the forgiveness group. After they filled out the first set of questionnaires, they were told to either stay and begin the first class or return home because they were in the comparison group. The people in the forgiveness class met weekly for six consecutive weeks with twelve to fifteen other people. Each class lasted an hour.

I had five goals for this experiment. The first was to help the forgiveness group participants feel less hurt about the situation that had brought them into the study. This was successfully accomplished, with a large reduction in hurt from the beginning of the study to the end. The subjects were asked to draw a line that would indicate on a scale from 1 to 10 how hurt they felt at that time. The forgiveness group initially rated their hurt at above 8 on the scale. At the end of the experiment—ten weeks after the forgiveness training ended—the forgiveness group rated their hurt as just a little over 3 on the same scale.

The second goal of my study was to help the participants learn to forgive as a general problem-solving strategy. I wanted them not only to forgive the person who hurt them but to put forgiveness on their menu of choices for dealing with future hurts. We devised brief descriptions of different situations that could elicit forgiveness, reconciliation, revenge, or a host of other responses. Examples ranged from being lied to by a close friend, having something stolen from one's home, experiencing a lover's departure without notice, or being the victim of unfair treatment at work. We asked participants to select from a range of choices, and we scored the number of forgiveness responses.

To further assess forgiveness, we created a vignette that described a hurtful interpersonal situation. In one scenario, a lover calls and says that he/she slept with his/her ex and wants to talk. Study participants had to describe their strategies for working through the pain and difficulty generated by this hypothetical situation. On both of these measures the students in the forgiveness group showed that they had learned to forgive. The students in the forgiveness group had better strategies for dealing with their pain and were more confident that they could forgive their lover.

The third goal of my training was to help participants forgive the person who had hurt them. Results varied on this. When measured one way, the study participants said they were more likely to forgive the offender. When measured another way, only the women students (75 percent of the study participants) forgave the offender sooner than the comparison group did.

The fourth goal of the training was to improve the psychological, emotional, and spiritual functioning of those in the forgiveness group. On each and every test the forgiveness group improved significantly relative to the comparison group. In other words, learning to forgive helped the forgiveness group members become emotionally healthier. It may be that becoming emotionally stronger is an important by-product of learning to forgive. When we are able to forgive, we feel more confident and optimistic. The hurt felt by the people in the comparison group lessened over time, but their psychological and emotional functioning did not improve.

The fifth goal of my forgiveness training was to reduce the anger held by the forgiveness group participants. I was specifically interested in reducing student's angry reactions to pain caused by their relationship with another person. I accomplished this goal: the forgiveness group members reduced their levels of anger by about 15 percent from the start of training to the final test ten weeks after the training ended. The students showed less anger both on the particular days they were tested and in how they responded to situations over the long term.

After the success of this first study, my dissertation adviser, Dr. Carl Thoresen, and I obtained a grant to redo and expand my forgiveness study. The grant enabled us to recruit more than 260 people for what remains the largest forgiveness study ever completed. Again, we measured study participants at the beginning of the experiment, at the end of the training, and at a follow-up evaluation eighteen weeks later.

In the Stanford Forgiveness Project, I worked with hurt adults between the ages of twenty-five and fifty. Again, I did not limit the nature of the offenses they had suffered, though I did exclude people who had been victims of abuse or assault within the last five years. We recruited people who were unable to forgive their spouse for cheating on them or for having alcohol or drug problems and people who were struggling to forgive best friends who had abandoned them, parents who had mistreated them, business partners who had lied to them, or siblings who didn't care about them. Again, we randomized people into forgiveness and comparison groups, and we measured participants' spiritual well-being, physical health, and levels of hurt, anger, stress, optimism, and forgiveness.

The results showed that the forgiveness group felt less stressed because of the training. Participants became more forgiving of the person who hurt them and more forgiving in general. These results held steady eighteen weeks after the training ended.

The subjects of the Stanford Forgiveness Project became significantly less angry, both in how angry they felt at a specific moment and in the levels of anger they felt more generally. At both the end of their training and eighteen weeks later, they felt less hurt than the people in the comparison group. The subjects also became significantly more optimistic over the course of the experiment.

Each time we tested them we also asked our subjects to rate their health on a scale of 1 to 5, with 1 signifying "great" and 5 "poor." Interestingly, all the participants had rated their health as very good when they began the study, yet the forgiveness group participants still reported a small improvement in their health. Finally, we asked the participants to indicate which common body responses to stress they regularly experienced—headaches, stomachaches, dizziness, tiredness, muscle aches, and so on. Learning to forgive significantly reduced the number of physical symptoms the forgiveness group felt. Clearly the forgiveness training not only allowed people to experience less mental stress but also lessened the effect of stress on their bodies.

Both of these research projects showed positive changes due to forgiveness. The studies were limited, however, in that we recruited subjects who had a grudge against someone close to them but not subjects who had suffered from an extreme example of a grievance. In my next two projects, I completely shifted my focus and recruited people who had suffered the greatest of tragedies: the loss of a close family member to murder.

Byron Bland, a Presbyterian minister, initially contacted me after hearing about the Stanford Forgiveness Project and my efforts to teach people to forgive. He had read newspaper accounts of my research and wondered whether my forgiveness training would work in Northern Ireland. Obviously Northern Ireland has many people who are in dire need of recovering from personal pain as a result of years of religiously and politically motivated violence. Byron knew that the pain from these tragedies was doing huge harm to individuals, families, and communities, and he asked me to try my forgiveness training with people from Northern Ireland.

Each of the five women we recruited for the first project had lost a son to murder, some as long as twenty years before. We found that the women still suffered tremendous pain no matter how long ago it was that their son had been murdered. Their suffering was increased by a feeling that their pain and need to heal had been ignored.

Political violence affects the rich and also the poor, as in this case. None of the women we wanted to help could afford the airfare from Ireland or had the resources to pay for accommodations at Stanford. They were from working-class families and simply did not have enough money to take a weeklong trip to America. Luckily, we were able to obtain cash donations for the plane fare and food, and each of the women was housed in a volunteer's home. After Stanford University agreed to provide us with space to conduct the workshops, we were able to begin the project and the women soon arrived at San Francisco International Airport.

We used the same techniques with the Irish women that we had used in the previous study groups. At our first meeting, they filled out questionnaires, and they did so again before they returned to Northern Ireland. Six months after leaving California, they completed a final set of questionnaires. At the beginning of the week, when the women measured their hurt, the average score was near 8.5 out of 10. At the end of the week, they had improved significantly—their feelings of hurt had gone down to 3.5. When I got their final results back six months later, the women still showed good results, scoring only 4 out of 10. These women showed very similar results to those I had obtained in my two previous studies. This astonished me—after all, their wounds were much more grievous than those of the people I had previously studied. They also showed a real improvement in their stress levels, with a reduction of almost half from the beginning of the training to the follow-up six months later.

The Irish women were able to forgive the murderer of their loved one roughly 40 percent more over the week of the training. This result remained constant at the follow-up evaluation. They also felt less depressed about their loss: when we measured their depression, they went from an average score of 17 out of 30 at the beginning of training to 7 out of 30 at the end of the training and 10 at the six-month follow-up.

The women had also become significantly more optimistic by the follow-up period. The only measure that didn't significantly change was their level of anger, which showed a decrease of about 25 percent from the beginning to the end of the experiment.

The positive effect of the Northern Ireland project exceeded our expectations. We started with women who understandably felt extremely hurt and very angry in their grief. We ended with women who mourned the loss of their children but, through forgiveness, had gained a measure of strength with which to cope. One of the women told me that she now realized that "life is for the living." Another woman said that she and the other mothers "must move on with the memory of our sons in our hearts."

It is truly impressive to me that these women improved so much, and in every way that we tested them. I'm thrilled that the forgiveness training worked for them and that the positive effects lasted even after they returned to a political climate that still pitted neighbor against neighbor.

Six months after our first Northern Ireland project ended, Byron Bland and I decided to set up another round of the Irish project. We had proved that our research could be effective with five people, but would our approach work with three or four times that many? Our methods were clearly effective with mothers who had lost children, but would they work if we invited other family members? We were also interested in discovering whether the methods that worked so well with women would be equally effective with both men and women attending the same sessions.

In this second project, the original five women returned to Stanford for another week of forgiveness training, and each one brought a couple of friends and family or community members who had also lost a loved one to violence. Our original women

,participated again, but they also helped guide their friends and family by using the forgiveness skills they had already learned. Our second group included young men whose fathers had been killed, women whose husbands had been murdered, and people whose siblings had died in bombings and assassinations.

Their stories were incredibly painful to hear. One man told of the loss of his father, who had been shot when he was only a young boy; he had grown up missing his father terribly, with only his mother and his brother at home. The only reason his father had been killed was because he was a Protestant. As a result, this young man hated Catholics with a passion. Amazingly, this intense anger dissolved to a large degree during the forgiveness work. He was able to see that the Catholics who had lost a family member grieved as much as he did. The pain of loss transcended the religious and political boundaries.

A young woman told us about the murder of her husband. He was kidnapped from his home and forced to drive a van loaded with explosives to a military checkpoint. The terrorists detonated the bomb as he sat in the driver's seat. Another woman recounted how her husband was murdered while babysitting their grandchildren. A third woman's husband had been murdered almost thirty years before, after which their house was bombed. The sheer number of these stories of cruel and senseless behavior made me start to feel numb.

In the second Irish project, we again provided a week of forgiveness training. Over the course of the week, we met as a group twice a day. Once again, we measured the results of the training at the end of the week before our subjects went home to Northern Ireland. This second Irish group also showed a dramatic improvement. The levels of hurt and pain they felt went down to the same level at which the first Irish group had ended. They were also significantly less depressed and angry.

With the second group we added a new question: we asked them to report on their physical well-being. How often did they experience physical symptoms of stress or emotional distress, such as headaches, nausea, sore muscles, and trouble falling asleep? At the end of the week, they reported feeling almost 35 percent fewer physical symptoms.

We also asked them about their energy and vitality levels. We were curious about how well they slept and whether they had a good appetite, felt energized, or suffered from aches and pains or were stiff and sore. At the end of the week, the group reported that they felt much more physically vital and that they had experienced an all-around improved sense of well-being.

Over the course of a week, a group of individuals who had suffered grievous losses were able to feel better both emotionally and physically. Our subjects could finally let go of their grief and move on in their lives with love. By doing this, they benefited hugely in both mind and body.

The last question we asked was perhaps the most important. We wanted to know the degree to which they had forgiven the person who murdered their son, brother, or father. Their answers offered up some interesting and provocative results. Two of the seventeen participants had become much less forgiving from the beginning of the week to the end. For some reason, the renewed attention to the murder of their loved one had made them feel angrier toward the murderer. However, the other fifteen members of our study felt more forgiving toward the killer who had taken their loved one.

This somewhat mixed result makes a lot of sense. Some people are bound to feel worse after spending seven days revisiting a horrible part of their life. I am delighted that a majority of the participants used the week to become more forgiving. Besides becoming more forgiving, the members of the group also became less depressed, hurt, and angry and felt better physically. They demonstrated the incredible power of human beings to heal from even the most awful horrors. The results reinforced my belief that I could teach people to forgive and that forgiveness is itself healing.

Two other researchers have had interesting results after using my methodology as a basis for their work. In the first study, an eight-week course of forgiveness training was given to subjects recruited from a cardiology practice in Florida. The results showed that people who were considered "angry" could reduce their high blood pressure by undergoing the training. Not only did their blood pressure improve, but they were less angry after the eight weeks. The subjects of the second study were premenopausal women, and the results showed that forgiveness training could reduce their levels of stress chemicals.

The next stage of my work is focused on bringing forgiveness training into the workplace. I hope that my work can make forgiveness a normal response to all kinds of difficult human interactions in everyday life, not just a response reserved for when a disaster occurs. For the last five years my two partners, Dr. Rick Aberman and Arthur DeLorenzo, and I have conducted an ongoing series of experiments. Our work focuses on using forgiveness as a general problem-solving strategy to reduce stress and increase productivity. Our first subjects were financial service advisers who were struggling with emotional distress after the stock market downturn in 2001. We wanted to see whether we could help these people be more productive at work and experience greater quality of life by training them in emotional competence, emphasizing forgiveness as a key ingredient.

So far we have completed our work with six groups of salespeople, and we have seen great results with them. The first four projects lasted a full year, while the next two were conducted over six months. The groups started with a one-day workshop teaching our subjects emotional competence and forgiveness. We then followed up with regular telephone coaching support. In between the workshop and the phone calls, we created a development plan for each participant based on improving his or her areas of weakness. The participants who got our training (as opposed to the control group) showed a 24 percent increase in sales from the beginning of the project to the end.

The productivity of the participants who did not receive training showed a 10 percent growth in sales during that same period of time. This means that our participants were selling at two and a half times the rate of the other people they worked with—a significant improvement. In addition to enhanced productivity, our group reported feeling much less stressed and much more positive at the end of our project. The benefits spilled over into other areas as well: our subjects' quality of life improved 10 percent, while they were 13 percent less angry. They also reported feeling physically better during this period. Our sixth and seventh six-month studies are currently under way, and we look forward to more revealing results in this area.

I have two more exciting forgiveness projects in the works. Over the past couple of years, I have conducted forgiveness trainings for numerous teachers, counselors, and therapists who work with at-risk adolescents in Hawaii. We want to see how forgiveness training can help both the adolescents and the people who care for them. In 2008 I will be training about 220 providers of youth services from multiple islands. Once the initial training is over, we'll pick one group of about 40 providers. We will then examine the effect of forgiveness training on the service providers for at-risk high school students and on the students themselves. We hope that the Hawaii project, which is being sponsored by the state, will help to make forgiveness training part of the overall curriculum.

I am also working on a project to provide forgiveness training to HIV-positive Latino men. The hope is that we can reduce the psychological distress caused by the disease and increase their ability to cope with it. I am working closely with researchers from the University of Texas, and we are using the techniques I've already talked about to help these men. Our pilot project is in development and will launch in 2008. I look forward to seeing the effect of my training on a different group of at-risk individuals.

Forgiveness in Relationships

Although the research specifically on forgiveness in relationships is limited, forgiveness research is a fast-growing field, and I am confident that research in this area will bloom as forgiveness becomes a mainstream concept over the next ten years. In this outline of the latest studies, we can see that they all seem to point to the need for forgiveness as a cornerstone for loving and lasting relationships.

A recent study proved that forgiveness in romantic relationships is directly related to the levels of satisfaction with and commitment to the relationship that both partners feel. Being forgiving helped both the forgiver and the forgiven feel better about the relationship.[10] Another study revealed that people whose first reaction to a relationship problem is to consider revenge have greater difficulty maintaining a close relationship.[11]

John Gottman did some interesting research on the factors that lead couples to divorce. His work showed that a marriage is in trouble when harshness, stonewalling, defensiveness, criticism, and contempt overtake it.[12] When these kinds of negative inter-actions start to occur regularly, the marriage is in danger and divorce starts to become more likely. Gottman's research also shows that a certain amount of conflict and disagreement is inevitable in a relationship and that many of a couple's disagreements will remain unresolved. If disagreements are inevitable in a relationship, then it is up to the couple to choose how they respond to them. It seems to me that a couple can either choose bitterness, which may well lead to divorce, or forgive each other and work to save their marriage.

Nobody knows for sure what makes a successful marriage. Many studies have tried to figure out why people stay married. The qualities that come up the most are shared religious and moral values, commitment and loyalty to each other, good communication, and shared affection. However, there is no definitive list of ingredients that can be mixed together to guarantee marital success. Once we start to broaden the factors for success, we find that forgiveness is on many of the lists, sometimes filed under a more inclusive heading such as loyalty or communication. One study found that forgiveness is one of the ten most important characteristics of a successful long-term marriage.[13] Another study of successful first marriages found that willingness to forgive and to be forgiven is one of the leading signs that a marriage will last.[14]

One study did an interesting examination of what is known as the three-stage model of forgiveness. It showed that couples who are in true forgiveness (stage three) have more successful marriages and a greater sense of well-being than those in false forgiveness (stage one).[15] Other studies have proven that married couples who understand and practice forgiveness are better at conflict resolution.[16] Clearly forgiveness can have a positive effect on the resolution and minimization of conflict in marriage.

One of the most important ways in which a couple can use forgiveness to create an enduring marriage is to repair their relationship after an affair. A recent dissertation found that forgiveness could be both part of the reason couples stay together and a result of their staying together.[17] Another small study recommended that forgiveness be taught in order to help couples recover from an affair.[18] A third study looked at how individuals whose lover or spouse had cheated handled the situation. The findings showed that if they felt forgiveness, it soothed the hostility that would have otherwise led to the end of the relationship. Compared to those who remained in their marriage, those individuals who chose to end the relationship after discovering their partner's cheating said that they felt less forgiving.[19]

Some of the most interesting and successful research in the usefulness of forgiving in a troubled relationship was done by Mark Rye, a professor at the University of Dayton. In his studies, he focused on divorced people, whom he taught to be more forgiving of their ex-spouses. Many divorced people strongly feel that they were mistreated by their partner, and consequently they harbor feelings of anger and hostility toward their ex long after the divorce has been finalized. Holding on to these negative feelings can cause many problems. The conflict between divorced parents is often very hurtful and damaging to their children. The parents may also find that their physical and psychological health suffers as a direct result of holding on to these negative emotions.

Rye and his colleagues were also interested in how different kinds of forgiveness intervention could work.[20] They put 149 divorced individuals into either a secular forgiveness group, a religiously integrated forgiveness group, or a comparison group that received no help. As in the other tests I've described, tests of forgiveness and mental health were administered before the groups began, one week after they ended, and six weeks later for a final follow-up. Participants in both intervention groups, compared to those in the comparison group, reported feeling significantly more forgiving toward an ex-spouse and had an improved understanding of forgiveness. Participants in the secular group said that they felt significantly less depressed as compared to the comparison group. Overall the people who had been in the two active groups said that they benefited greatly in a wide variety of ways.

Douglas Kelley, a professor of communication studies at Arizona State University, wanted to find out how exactly communication works in fostering forgiveness in romantic relationships. He and his colleagues used three studies to look at how forgiveness is communicated within romantic relationships, most specifically marriage, and what kind of impact these communication strategies have on the relationship. He first looked at interviews with sixty long-term married couples who talked about giving and receiving forgiveness in their own marriages. Specifically, they addressed why they forgave, how they forgave, and the importance of forgiveness in maintaining a marriage over time. The second and third studies looked at couples who talked about times when they had used forgiveness in their relationships.

One final note on the research about forgiveness in relationships. Although many couples therapists feel positively about forgiveness, they do not use it as part of their therapy because they do not have sufficient training to provide step-by-step instruction to distressed clients in how to practice forgiveness.[21] Some try, but most do not have the tools to be helpful. I was given little to no help myself in this regard. I am hoping this book will provide the missing link for therapists and individuals to help them bring forgiveness into their lives and relationships.

FOUR

The Four Stages of Forgiveness

There is a difference between forgiving something specific your partner has done and becoming a forgiving person in your relationship. Do you only forgive things like your partner forgetting to walk the dog, or do you forgive the parts of your partner's personality that would drive any normal person crazy? Both kinds of forgiveness are important in a successful marriage, but becoming more and more forgiving toward your partner is critical. Forgiving a specific wrong reduces the stress and hostility that stems from an unresolved hurt, but becoming a truly forgiving husband or wife creates a marriage that surpasses what you ever hoped it could be. When you decide to really forgive your partner, you create an opening into a deep and sustaining love. Experiencing and giving that deep love is what we all crave when we enter into a relationship. That love is what we deny ourselves when we spend our lives criticizing our lovers and complaining about all the ways in which they do not measure up to our standards.

This book is devoted to helping you become a more forgiving partner, and it is also a road map to making you a better lover. Love is what happens when you stop creating stress by arguing about the imperfections of the person you married. That does not mean you like everything your spouse does or that you don't talk to your spouse about things. You are still going to have specific problems that require forgiveness, but thankfully those will be rare. Forgiveness allows the love to flourish and to not be corroded by your resentments and complaints.

It is the smaller annoyances, and our negative responses to them, that kill happiness between partners. That criticism can quickly build into resentment. We take a normal flawed human being and turn him or her into a problem by being negative. We find faults in the way she dresses, her bathroom habits, or the way she does not listen to us. We critique his friends, how he relates to his parents, the junk he watches on TV, or his taste in wine. Our lover is bound to have numerous qualities that are not up to our standards, and reacting to them negatively can make us distant and critical. Distance and criticism can erode love and goodwill in both partners, and over time it spells death for the relationship.

Stress-related disease isn't caused by the big problems such as divorce, loss of a job, or the murder of a loved one; it's the little daily hassles that can really hurt us. That is because throughout the course of our lives we encounter only a few big problems. What causes most of our stress is the accumulation of little problems and irritations that we do not handle well. We don't realize that these small but chronic problems are harming us, so we do not put the energy into working them out. These daily hassles, however, appear to be more of a health risk than the occasional big issue that comes our way. This is true in relationships as well. It is our inability to let go of the daily relationship hassles that causes the most decay in our relationship, not the infrequent big disasters.

Jack was having problems with forgiving his girlfriend Laurie. He was angry with her for coming home late twice in one week, and he was also having problems being forgiving toward her in general. A more forgiving attitude would have allowed him to both forgive her for being late and avoid taking offense at her lateness in the first place. When I suggested to Jack that taking offense at what Laurie did was optional and that his doing so actually added little to his ability to get along with her, he took it as a radical notion. Jack wanted Laurie to be on time so that he could help them build a successful life together. He found it hard to make any kind of plans for them when he didn't know what time she would be back. Jack would have found it more helpful to talk to her about the issue rather than automatically take offense at it. Taking offense means that what Laurie did personally bothered Jack and he was offended by her actions. In actuality, the only thing Laurie did was arrive home later than Jack wanted.

There are three components to the process by which we take our lover's no and turn it into a long-standing hurt or grudge:

1. Taking an exaggerated level of personal offense

2. Blaming our partner for how we feel

3. Creating a grievance story

By nurturing these three things, we keep our wounds alive much longer than the initial no we received. Jack could have chosen to notice that Laurie was late, understood that he needed to talk to her, and decided that that was the end of the issue. He did not have to be mad because she was late. He could have been happily living with a woman who came home later than expected a couple of times a week. By taking offense at her action, he lengthened and intensified the grief cycle more than was necessary. His response to her lateness provides a great example of how a lover can take disappointment and turn it into love-eroding contempt, which is what kills relationships. Forgiveness is what allows the Jacks and Lauries of this world to stay in love and keep their relationships alive.

Debbie was a case in point. The grievance story she was telling about her husband Sal kept her stuck in the wounds of her marriage. The facts did not change: Sal was a difficult man to live with. He did not listen well, was sarcastic, and ignored her in social situations. He worked hard, was generally tired when at home, and yet did his chores around the house. Debbie would point out what she did not like, and each time Sal would swear he would never do it again. Debbie got legitimately frustrated with their interactions but thought the only way he would change was to nag him. So nag she did, and their marriage was a difficult one.

To make things worse, Debbie told everyone she met what an unfeeling louse she was married to. She would call her friends to tell them every time Sal did not meet her expectations, and she described in minute detail how uncommunicative he was. She took what her husband did personally and then blamed him for her distress and unhappiness. Debbie felt angry, abandoned, lonely, and scared, and she felt that these feelings were Sal's fault. Blame is not the same as asking someone to change his behavior. By blaming Sal, Debbie gave him responsibility for how hurt and angry she was. Since she often felt bad, that gave Sal an enormous amount of power and made Debbie feel small and helpless. Debbie worsened the situation by creating a hostile grievance story about Sal's failings and how helpless she felt. She told this story over and over.

Every time Debbie complained about her husband her stomach would hurt and her body would tense. That is the sort of thing that happens when we blame other people for our physical and emotional experience. To Debbie, her suffering was Sal's fault. Like many of the people I work with, Debbie did not know how to deal with her disappointment without complaining about her partner. Debbie felt that if she constantly complained about Sal and let everyone know what a louse he was, then she would not be held responsible for their marital woes. The temporary glee she felt when recounting her travails was dwarfed by the power it gave her husband to make her miserable. Rather than successfully resolving her marital troubles, Debbie remained fully in her husband's thrall—a helpless victim of unkindness and lack of care.

Through forgiveness training, however, she recognized that the repetition of her grievance story only increased the power her husband had over her. If she wanted their life to improve, she would have to do more than be angry and full of blame: she would have to forgive Sal. What Debbie learned was that however many different ways her husband could be unkind to her (saying no to her requests), a grudge is always created in the same way. Debbie regularly and repeatedly took offense at her husband's actions. She blamed him all the time for how she felt, even when he was not with her, and she created a story of her relationship that hurt her every time she told it. None of these reactions to Sal's behavior were in fact his fault or responsibility.

Debbie had to decide whether Sal was a keeper and whether she wished to remain with him. She also had to learn to forgive him for what he had done and how he had treated her. Finally, if she was going to stay with him, Debbie had to forgive Sal for who he was. When she was able to do all three of these things, their conversations improved and their relationship started to grow. After a while Debbie learned that the basis for actually loving Sal was forgiving him for who he was. Sal was going to be himself, whether or not Debbie was around.

I hope that you also can learn to be more forgiving of your partner. Doing this will be worth whatever effort you have to make to get there. Even if you are able to develop a forgiving nature, however, you will still have specific offenses to work through. But being forgiving will reduce the number of obstacles you create in your marriage and improve the pleasure of the time you spend with your loved one.

No matter how perfectly loving your relationship is, your partner will do irritating things and make choices that are potentially dangerous to your relationship. Inevitably you will have to make decisions that may require difficult conversations. Forgiveness will help you have more peaceful conversations and help make the difficult decisions easier to think out. Both situational forgiveness (forgiving a specific act) and dispositional forgiveness (becoming a more forgiving person) can be practiced with specific techniques for getting over wounds and moving on. Most of the time the health of our marriages requires only that we be more forgiving of who our partner is. Some of our partner's actions may require specific acts of forgiveness because the resulting wound is so deep that the grief takes time to heal. The power of forgiveness is such that even situational forgiveness is easier the more forgiving we are in general.

The most direct way to bring the power of forgiveness into our lives is simply to be forgiving of our partners. We do this when we feel loving enough that we are rarely mad or negatively disposed toward them. We do not take offense when they are late or sloppy or inconsiderate or tired or grumpy. We simply give them the benefit of the doubt and appreciate them enough to minimize, not ignore, their flaws.

To make this type of forgiving more understandable, I need to explain the four stages of forgiveness. The four stages are a road map of the processes that people move through as they learn to forgive. They show that forgiveness helps to heal past hurts and also minimizes the possibility of creating present and future hurts.

By being forgiving, we can inoculate ourselves against being hurt. Having a forgiving nature is a powerful thing and can profoundly improve our relationships.

We are able to forgive because we have the ability to choose how we behave and act. When our lover lies to us, it is our choice how to deal with it. Paul reacted to lies by throwing things. Lisa reacted by running away from her husband, and Toni by hating her partner. The lie does not contain instructions for how you are respond to it. If your husband watches football each and every Sunday, there is no rule guiding how you respond. You don't have to storm over to the set and throw the remote. When your wife forgets to lock the front door, there is no automatic response expected of you. You can scream and yell, or you can choose to be less emotional about her mistake. You have the choice to forgive or not to forgive, and no one can force you to do either. If you want to forgive your wife, no one can stop you, no matter how poorly she may have acted. The choice to forgive or not is similar to the choices you make about how much anger you will express and how long you will hold a grudge.

Let's take this idea of choice one step further. If you have the option to forgive, then this suggests that you also have the option to take offense or not in the first place. One of the ways to hasten forgiveness is to take offenses less personally. I firmly believe that relationships would improve if people chose to take offense less often. Being more tolerant of your partner's bad behavior would do a lot to make him or her feel more accepted and loved. This in turn would make your partner more likely to treat you with kindness. You have a choice in how you react to your partner's bad behavior. Surely it makes sense to try to be more accepting and less prone to offense if doing so decreases the number of times you actually have to forgive your partner.

We all have to work at being more forgiving. The next few times your partner does something hurtful, try to practice forgiving him or her. Doing this will help you to become more forgiving toward your partner and will greatly improve your relationship. If your husband always forgets to clean up the bathroom, for instance, try to forgive his sloppiness the next time you notice it. After practicing forgiveness a few times, you may notice that you are less inclined to get angry at the other annoying things he does. You may well find that you are more patient with him when he leaves the soap out or fails to run errands as requested. Forgiveness—or the ability to live life without taking offense when you get a no and grieving your losses without blame—is a choice that can be practiced anytime. Although it's not the only positive response, forgiveness is a skillful way to deal with the "slings and arrows of outrageous fortune" or the ups and downs of every important relationship.

The Four Stages of Forgiveness

Couples go through four stages as they learn to forgive. The first stage starts with your partner controlling you through his or her power to hurt you. As you pass from stage one to stage four, you gain the power to control the degree of pain you feel when your partner is difficult. You do not gain control over your lover as much as you learn to control your emotional reactivity and your blood pressure. Forgiveness allows you to think more clearly, solve problems more wisely, and have greater access to loving feelings.

As you follow these steps, you will see that learning to forgive is more than just a wonderful way to resolve past hurts and grievances. Lovers learn to use forgiveness to limit their chance of getting hurt in the present as well as minimize the amount of time they remain hurt from the past.

Research shows that by healing the past, forgiveness can provide a more peaceful present.

Now I will show you how to use forgiveness to heal your marriage in ways you may not have anticipated. Try to think of the process of finding forgiveness as being like tuning an old-fashioned analog radio. The first step in tuning the radio is deciding that you want to listen to a particular station. The first time you get the station may be by accident. Maybe you were going through all the stations on the dial and heard a snippet of a song you liked. Finding that station again can be hard if the signal is not strong or if you have never practiced tuning your radio. Think of this station as your forgiveness channel, and the snippet of song as a happy memory of briefly being in tune with your loved one. If you can find a way to stay tuned to that forgiveness station, you are more likely to have a constant, harmonious background noise that enables you and your spouse to communicate easily.

To find the station again you will have to adjust your dial and go back to where you heard the station originally. At first the station may be hard to distinguish, but with practice you can find the frequency you want. It may take awhile to fine-tune the station, but when you are certain you have the right wavelength, you can leave the dial set there. Whenever you turn on your radio, you will hear this station. Starting with this station does not stop you from finding other stations. There will be times when the music is better on other parts of the dial, and there will be times when you are not in the mood for this one station. As you fine-tune the forgiveness channel, less and less static and interference get in the way.

In the first stage of forgiveness, a loss in your life has caused you to experience anger and hurt, and you feel justified in your negative feelings. The hurt or angry people whose stories are told in this book all started at this stage of forgiveness. Darlene was very angry at her husband's infidelity. She felt that his actions were wrong, that she was relatively blameless, and that his infidelity caused her emotional distress. She told anyone who would listen how awful she felt and how poorly her husband had behaved.

At stage one of forgiveness, you are filled with self-justified anger and hurt. You feel mad at or hurt by your ex or your present lover for something that person has done to you. In your mind, he or she is responsible for how bad you feel. When you think about the situation, you blame your partner's actions for your unhappiness, not your response to them. What you don't realize is that you can choose how to react. You might also be so wounded that you are convinced it would be wrong to forgive the offense. At stage one, there is usually both active and submerged anger as well as a great deal of pain. Darlene's story, like the stories of others who were hurt and had not healed, can be read as a howl of pain.

The second stage of forgiveness begins when you realize that the hurt and anger filling your life after a betrayal feels bad. You may become concerned about your emotional balance or physical health, or you may start to wonder how the grief you feel is affecting your overall happiness and well-being. After living with the pain for a while, you may begin to think about how to repair the damage to the relationship. Or you may simply decide that you have thought about the wrong done to you enough and it is time to move on. Through trial and error, you find ways to move on with less bitterness.

In the second stage, you take steps to lessen the impact of the grievance on your life. John tried thinking about their problem from his wife's point of view, and this helped him make peace with her. Jackie decided to ignore her husband when he said certain things, and by doing this she came to realize that her husband's words were not that big of a deal. Philip learned to calm himself down and not take it personally when his wife was too stressed to pay attention to him. No matter what strategy you use, after an extended period you are no longer actively aggrieved. After ignoring her husband's hurtful words for a while, Jackie was happy to tell her friends that she had let go of much of her hurt and anger toward her husband.

In the second stage of forgiveness, you start to notice that your bad feelings are not helping you and in fact are making things worse. You start to realize that you must take steps to prevent yourself from suffering any further emotional pain. By taking control of your emotional and physical unhappiness, you are able to disentangle yourself from the wrongdoer and take control of your own life again.

When Susan's husband Barry told her that he was tired of hearing about her terrible childhood, her first reaction was to get angry with him. She immediately decided he was a jerk and called her friend Donna for affirmation.

Later, when Susan had calmed down, she asked Barry why he had said that to her. He responded that Susan saw her mother only twice a year, yet obsessed about her in a way that was out of proportion to their relationship. It was at this point that Susan started forgiveness training. She learned the forgiveness methods that allowed her to see clearly what her husband was saying. Even more important, Susan was able to really think about her own life and finally understand how she had been affected by the difficult and painful relationship she had with her mother when she was young.

In the third stage of forgiveness, you concentrate on how good it can feel to forgive. By focusing on the last time you forgave—whether it was fifteen minutes ago or two years ago—you remember that forgiving can help you move on and feel better. In the third stage of forgiveness, you can use the forgiveness techniques you will learn in this book as soon as you start to feel a grudge forming and thus challenge your bad habits on the spot. By doing this, you will prevent your partner's failings from taking up a lot of space in your own mind. The third stage of forgiveness comes after you have seen the results of forgiveness in action and you are able to choose to let go of your anger over a loved one's wrongdoing.

In this stage, you deliberately choose to feel the hurt you have experienced for a shorter period. You know from experience that your negative feelings will pass. Instead of dwelling on your anger, you realize that your feelings contain truths about your life. Your feelings are trying to tell you that some action is necessary to heal yourself or your relationship.

You also realize that there is only a certain amount of space in your mind. You can choose to use that space to dwell in anger or to work at repairing the relationship and eventually letting go of the problematic situation. Instead of using that space to grieve and feel anger, you use that space to work on a solution. You decide to forgive because you have practiced forgiveness and see its clear benefits in your life. This stage can be reached in a relationship whether the problem is the damage from an affair, difficult in-laws, or conflicts over sex or parenting. Stage three is about taking control over your own feelings and choices.

At this stage of forgiveness, you realize that the length of time you suffer because of your partner's wrongdoing is up to you. Susan was an excellent example of a person at this stage. She decided that the next time her lover hurt her she was going to work hard to prevent it from becoming a grievance. She also decided that she was not going to allow herself to become depressed because of the deliberate provocations of her mother or anyone else. In this stage of forgiveness, Susan realized that she could control how long she spent angry and hurt. She made the decision to work hard to minimize the length of time she felt hurt and angry. With practice, she was successful.

The fourth stage of forgiveness is the most difficult and arguably the most powerful. At this stage, you simply become a forgiving person and make a habit of practicing forgiveness with your lover. This stage comes when you make the decision to forgive first and let as many of the troubling things go as you can. As a forgiving person, you become resistant to taking offense even when, for instance, your wife spends too much time with the children and not enough with you. Your skin becomes tougher. You take less personal offense. You take responsibility for your own feelings, and you talk about your relationships in ways that focus on good intentions, both your own and those of the people in your life.

The fourth stage of forgiveness is about choosing not to be hurt in the first place, even if your loved one neglects to do the things he or she promised to do. This does not mean that you condone unkindness or become a doormat; you can stand up for yourself and still be forgiving. What it does mean is that you save your feelings of hurt and anger for when they are truly needed. In other words, you have learned not to take hurtful actions so personally and not to blame the offender for how you are feeling, but you can still accept that sometimes your partner simply crosses the line. At stage four, you understand that your partner is not perfect and will hurt you occasionally.

At this stage, you understand that other people, including those you live with, may hurt you, so there is no surprise when it happens. With this understanding, you can prepare yourself to forgive before any wrongdoing occurs. You do not have to wait for your girlfriend to forget again to pick up the mail or buy the milk.

Stage four is usually reached at the same time you come to some or all of the following ways of thinking about offenses:

- I want to waste as little of my life as possible in the pain caused by anger and hurt. I want to react well when things do not go the way I want in my marriage. This decision will allow me to forgive myself, forgive my partner, and even forgive life itself when necessary.

- Love comes with positive and negative experiences. I can't expect to have only good things come my way. Instead, I hope for the good and know I can forgive the bad.

- Dealing with relationships is a challenge. I want to be a survivor and not a victim. Each hurtful situation challenges my determination to live as fully and lovingly as possible. I accept the challenges that life sends my way.

- I know it hurts when my partner does not forgive me. I do not want to hurt him/her in this way, so I will look at the problem in such a way that I can either deal with it successfully or let it go.

- Love is filled with beauty and wonder. I am missing these experiences if I am constantly replaying old offenses in my head. I forgive myself for letting my grudges temporarily sidetrack me from appreciating life.

- My husband/wife does the best he/she can. When he/she makes a mistake, the best way to help is by offering understanding. The first step in this process is to forgive whatever he/she did that was wrong.

- I am not perfect. How can I expect my partner to be?

- I understand that everyone, myself included, operates primarily out of self-interest. I expect that sometimes I, in my self-interest, will be hurt by my lover's own expression of self-interest. When I understand that this is an ordinary part of life, what is there to be upset about? When I grasp that self-interest is my guiding principle, how can I not offer forgiveness to both my partner and myself for behaving that way?

These insights are all examples of stage four forgiveness, but they are not the only ways in which you can become a forgiving person. You can develop your own way of thinking about your marriage or relationship. As you read through the book, I will give you many strategies to help you through the pain of stages two and three and ultimately help you create a stage four relationship. You have probably had good relationships in which you were able to think like this in the past; you probably know successfully married people who are at stage four forgiveness now. These marriages include the understanding that both partners will make mistakes in their relationship. By accepting this reality, the couple is able to put their energy into solving the problems rather than getting angry, blaming each other, and creating grievance stories.

The first part of stage four forgiveness is learning to think like a forgiving person. Practicing forgiveness every day is another crucial component. You do not have to wait for someone to hurt you badly in order to practice forgiveness. Practicing forgiveness allows you to develop forgiveness muscles in the same way that going to the gym develops physical muscles. Forgiveness muscles must be worked out regularly, just like your biceps or abs, in order to grow strong and reliable.

As you work toward stage four forgiveness, pay attention to the small slights you experience daily and practice with them. For example, if you are in the twelve-items-or-less checkout line at your supermarket and you see two people ahead of you with eighteen or so items in their carts, ask yourself: how will I respond? Notice that you have a range of choices.

One possible response is to get mad at the people who have too many items. You can choose to be rude and aggressive toward them and the checkout person who let them stay in the line. Another response is to feel angry but to try to ignore the situation and read a magazine. Alternatively, you can turn to the person behind you and pointedly complain about the selfishness of people who don't care to follow the rules. Or you can use the supermarket line as an opportunity to forgive the people who are in line with extra items. When you practice forgiveness in this way, forgiveness becomes available when you really need it.

Another powerful way to practice forgiveness is to remind yourself that other people do not always have your best interest at heart. Once you start to think about this idea, you have to accept that you yourself do not always act in the best interest of others, not even the best interest of your husband or wife. Taking this perspective, you understand that it is inevitable that even people in love will hurt each other. Since this is true in all relationships, you will have many opportunities' to practice forgiveness.

For example, Harry and Sue had allowed Sue's parents to move in with them. Sue's mom had been uptight and nasty all week because she was worried about her hospitalized husband. She was short with Harry and Sue and did not notice their efforts to be kind and understanding toward her. She snapped at both of them and was impatient with their kids. In one sense, Harry was justified in being upset at his mother-in-law. She and her husband had lived with Harry and Sue rent-free for three years and benefited from all that Harry and Sue did to help them. However, Harry could also have looked at the situation from another point of view and asked himself: what is the big deal? His mother-in-law's mind was on her sick husband and her own fears and struggles, not on Harry's feelings.

Harry and his mother-in-law were both guided by their self-interest. Harry's mother-in-law's absolute priority was her husband's health, not her son-in-law's feelings. Harry likewise prioritized his own feelings over those of his mother-in-law. Harry could choose to forgive his mother-in-law by understanding his own self-interest for what it was. He cared more about himself and expected his family to do the same. His mother-in-law cared more about her sick husband and less about Harry's feelings. In cases like this, when your priorities are different from those of the people around you, forgiveness can soothe your hurt feelings and allow you to maintain functioning relationships.

Another useful point to remember is that disappointments, hurts, and wounds occur in all stable long-term marriages and that differing expressions of self-interest are usually to blame. People inflict pain on their loved ones in all phases of relationships and in all kinds of loving families and friendships. Since, like people, every relationship has its good and bad points, our relationships give us almost unlimited opportunities to practice forgiveness—to try to take less offense and to prevent conflicts from escalating.

Sometimes your husband will hurt you because he wants to do what he wants to do and not what you want him to do. Most of the time we call that selfish, but sometimes it is simply people making their own decisions and acting in their own self-interest. Anna was hurt when her husband Dave decided to go skiing with his friends rather than visit her parents. The original plan had been for both of them to join the skiing party, but Anna decided not to go because her parents wanted company. Anna's relationship with her parents was a bone of contention with Dave: he felt that she regularly paid more attention to them than to him.

This time Anna had to drive the six hours to her parents' house alone. On the way her car broke down, and she was stranded on the roadside for three hours. She had to wait for the tow truck to get her and then for the repair shop to replace the part her car needed. By the end of all this, Anna was seriously pissed off at her husband. She thought he was selfish and inconsiderate for not being with her when she needed help. However, when Anna told me this story, I had to ask her why her husband was wrong for doing what he wanted rather than what Anna wanted. They were both adults, and Anna herself had made the choice to change her plans and do what she wanted to do. The truth about marriage is that the partners are both united and independent. Each spouse is allowed to make his or her own decisions, and doing so is not necessarily selfish.

Suppose Anna had forgiven her husband for his choice even before they left on their respective trips. When her car broke down, she would have already taken responsibility for her own feelings and saved herself a lot of grief and possibly a nasty showdown with Dave. She would have been able to forgive the fact that Dave had decided to spend his free time the way he wanted to rather than the way she wanted him to. By practicing forgiveness, she could have taken control of the situation and not been in the weaker position of feeling anger and resentment.

Forgiving Dave would not have meant that Anna had to stop asking him to join her on trips. Nor would forgiving Dave have meant that Anna liked the choices her husband made. By forgiving Dave, Anna would have stopped blaming her husband for her own feelings, taken ownership of those feelings, and accepted that she was visiting her parents because it was important to her. She and Dave could still have been loving, committed partners even if he did not care about visiting her parents. When you expect and allow people to be different, it becomes much easier for you to forgive them. Forgiving allows you to understand that what is right for you will not be right for everybody.

Sometimes people hurt you by not being available to you when you need or want them to be. Steve's wife Marjorie regularly fell asleep at 9:00 P.M. He was hurt by this habit of hers; as far as he was concerned, the night was young at nine o'clock, and he wanted her companionship. He wanted to make love and took her tiredness as a personal insult. Steve and Marjorie had very different schedules. Steve was a night owl and usually left for work late in the morning. He also did not need a lot of sleep. Marjorie cared for the couple's three young children and was up early with them. She was home all day caring for the two youngest children and working for Steve's business. Marjorie was not a night owl and needed at least seven hours of sleep every night. By nine at night, she could not keep her eyes open.

Each time Marjorie fell asleep, Steve felt hurt and rejected. He thought that if his wife cared for him, she would be available in the evening, when he was ready for her. His hurt feelings about her perceived rejection caused a major strain in their marriage. Marjorie tried hard to give Steve what she could within the limitations of their schedules. But imagine if instead of pouting and picking a fight, Steve had forgiven Marjorie's different sleep cycle and her exhaustion from caring for their three small children?

Sometimes a grievance is the result of someone's deliberate attempt to wound us. Often that person justifies wounding us as a response to a hurt we have inflicted on them. Steve and Marjorie's relationship was an example of this pattern of hurt. Marjorie often went upstairs to bed just to hurt her husband. She rejected him on purpose because he was so unforgiving of her tiredness. At other times she would keep the children up late just so that she would be unavailable to Steve. In Marjorie's mind, Steve deserved this treatment because of how insensitive and unkind he was to her.

Steve reacted by behaving even more selfishly and ragging on his wife relentlessly. He would gripe at her in the morning and again when he got home. He complained to his friends and family that Marjorie was uncaring, sexless, and unresponsive. In particular, Steve was sarcastic to his wife, and sometime he would wake Marjorie up just to start trouble. Steve justified his harsh treatment of Marjorie as a natural response to her inability to meet his needs. Both Marjorie and Steve gave themselves permission to be hurtful as a justified response to the other's actions.

Suppose that Steve and Marjorie had made a habit of forgiving each other, or that they were able to understand that hurt people tend to hurt right back. Imagine if each realized that the other's unkindness was a cry of pain. If Steve and Marjorie could only have accepted that the other's unkindness was triggered by pain instead of selfishness, they could have started to forgive each other. Once they were able to forgive each other's unkindness, they would naturally have wanted to be kind to each other and to spare each other further pain. Imagine if, instead of responding with cruelty, Steve and Marjorie had responded to each other with renewed affection that arose out of their forgiveness. In this situation, there would be many opportunities to practice forgiveness.

Finally, some of our wounds come about as the result of poor dumb luck. Sometimes we may just be in the wrong place at the wrong time. Anna had had her car checked out, but it still broke down two hundred miles from home while she was driving to see her parents. She then made a difficult situation worse by blaming Dave for not being there when she needed him. Anna forgot that accidents and car breakdowns can happen at any time. She didn't factor in that a car can break down even after it has been recently serviced. Imagine if Anna had forgiven Dave, forgiven her car, and simply enjoyed the experience as best she could. Imagine if she had understood what an ideal opportunity this was to practice forgiveness and how much forgiveness could help her.

Clark and Colette had been a couple for eight months, even though he lived in Denver and she lived in Los Angeles. He regularly flew out to visit her, and this weekend he was supposed to arrive in L.A. at 6:00 P.M. However, when Clark arrived at the Denver airport, he saw that a flight scheduled to depart earlier had been delayed. He ran all the way to the gate and was just able to get on a plane leaving two hours before his original flight was scheduled to depart. The new arrival time got him to Colette's house at four instead of six. Clark tried to call from the Denver airport to let her know, but her phone was busy.

When Clark arrived, Colette was surprised that he was so early and not entirely happy to see him. Colette worked at home and still had a few more tasks to get done. Clark was hurt by Colette's cool greeting, and his first response was to wonder why he had bothered to come see her. Colette felt guilty, but couldn't help being mad at Clark for disturbing her during business hours. She liked to pay full attention to her work until it was done, then relax and focus on her personal life instead.

Colette felt torn: she had work to do and a deadline to meet, but she also wanted to spend time with her boyfriend. She knew that Clark was demanding and required a lot of attention. In fact, it was Clark's demanding nature that had led her to ask him to arrive at 6:00 P.M. She wanted to have time to complete her work, take a shower, and sit down for a moment before he arrived. Clark had meant no harm when he boarded the earlier plane: he had simply had the opportunity to get in a few hours sooner, and that had seemed like a good thing. This innocent action led to bad feelings on both sides. All because of dumb luck happening to two people who were not practiced enough in forgiveness.

In stage four forgiveness, we understand how easy it is to hurt or be hurt by our loved one, and we take the opportunity to forgive whenever we can. Since we realize how easy it is to cause pain, we strive to bring peace to our relationship instead. Rather than blaming our partner, we look to give him or her the benefit of the doubt. Doing so does not make us a doormat: instead, we have become a person who understands the power of forgiveness and the tendency of people to hurt each other.

Once you have reached stage four, you understand that each person sees the world a little differently and that there are limitations to your own worldview. You understand that we all want slightly different things because we have had different experiences. Imagine life as if we were each watching our own particular movie. You are the star of that movie, and there are an infinite number of possible plot lines. The story and tone of your movie come from your past experiences, and it is filled with your hopes and dreams.

Now imagine the world as a huge multiplex theater complex with an enormous number of movies available. These theaters play all sorts of different films. Some people spend their time watching horror movies, while others prefer love stories. How does someone who has just watched a double feature of westerns communicate with someone who spent the afternoon indulging in sweet romantic comedies? We might struggle to talk with someone who watched such radically different movies and is probably feeling and experiencing completely different emotions.

Darlene was furious at her husband for leaving her. Her movie theater was showing only *Betrayal,* which was still in the middle of a long engagement there. Each time she watched the movie she hated the other leading character, her husband. Unfortunately, Darlene's husband was watching *Love Story,* not *Betrayal.* He was reveling in his exciting, passionate relationship with his new lover. He was enjoying the endless repeats of *Love Story* so much that it didn't even occur to him to wonder what was playing in Darlene's theater down the street.

People need to be able to forgive others for watching different movies. When I talk with people like Darlene, I ask them which movie they would like to watch over and over, *Betrayal* or *Love Story.* At stage four, you understand that other people are going to be watching different movies and having life experiences different from yours. If your husband is enjoying his film, he sure isn't going to stop at your cinema anytime soon. Instead of being angry, try to save your attention for those who sit down next to you at your theater and offer to share their popcorn.

You need to be able to talk to your partner even when he or she has watched a different movie from yours. It's tempting to simply criticize each other for going to different films, but you both need to make the effort to try to understand the story line and perspective of the other's movie. It's human to want your partner to listen to the plot of your movie, but when you are in a relationship, you need to be willing to hear your loved one's take on things and offer your understanding and perspective. When you and your partner watch *and* review each other's film, you show each other that you care and you avoid creating a grudge based in your different takes on life.

Amanda and Joe had been married for twenty-five years, but as they neared their fiftieth birthdays they realized that they were watching different movies. Joe was thinking of finally slowing down and working less. Amanda was done with raising their children and feeling bored working part-time at a low-wage job. Joe's movie was an exotic adventure tale that had them in Hawaii for an extended, relaxing vacation after a lifetime of hard work. Amanda's film couldn't have been more different. After a lifetime of low-prestige, low-income work, she wanted a demanding full-time job with the opportunity to make a sizable chunk of her own money—she was watching *Working Girl*. Neither Amanda nor Joe was willing to forgive the other for their different dreams. Both claimed to feel misunderstood and hurt and wondered if the marriage could be saved.

It took forgiveness training to help Joe and Amanda realize that they were at different life stages. In our sessions, they learned to ask each other about their long-term goals. Through forgiveness they realized that their ultimate goals were very much in line. However, they both came to understand that they might have to wait to get everything they wanted. As a first step, Amanda and Joe decided to take a long trip and then switch roles. Joe worked part-time and Amanda went back to the career she had put on hold long ago. They agreed to revisit their decision every year, with the understanding that their marriage had to be preserved.

Reaching stage four in forgiveness training is a sign that you have figured out that you have power over your feelings and that conflict is inevitable in any kind of relationship. It's also important to realize that you don't have to be at the same stage of forgiveness in all your relationships. This book is focused on helping you get to stage four in your committed love relationship, but you can apply the lessons to other relationships as well. There may be some people in your life for whom you feel such love that you are already at stage four: openhearted and ready to forgive. Many of you, for instance, already feel forgiving toward your children. Forgiving them does not mean that you approve of all that they do, but rather that you can acknowledge they have hurt you without making them your enemy. You have a reservoir of love to draw upon that allows you to forgive them. Once you forgive your children, you can let the insults go and work with them to resolve the problems.

Sometimes the hurt your lover has caused is so deep that you have no reservoir of goodwill to draw upon. It is possible to stay stuck at this stage for years. When you are in this situation, your well of goodwill for your lover is dry and you cannot imagine feeling openhearted toward him or her. *Forgive for Love* can help you through this stage by giving you the forgiveness tools to move on to stages two and three. Remember that when you have a committed love partner, you always have the choice to forgive. In stage two, you make a onetime choice to forgive in order to hurt less from something specific your lover did. When you reach stage three, you make a choice to forgive on a daily basis. At stage four, you become forgiving by nature, so that your choice is already made. You choose all the stages of forgiveness to hurt less and experience more peace and healing.

When I began my first forgiveness experiment almost ten years ago, I had two goals. One was to teach people to forgive those who had hurt them. The other goal was to help people use forgiveness to prevent future problems as well as heal existing hurts. I saw that my clients, friends, and family thought about forgiveness only when dealing with big hurts. They considered forgiveness something that was very hard to do, and by the time they thought about forgiveness it was usually too late. They had failed to practice forgiveness, and so their forgiveness muscles were flabby.

The idea behind my program was to develop a technique that would help people deal with both the big hurts and little hurts in life. I wanted to teach people to become more forgiving in general, not just to use forgiveness in specific instances. I have that same wish for you. If you put the lessons in this book into practice, you will find that you have the power to create a much happier and more harmonious relationship than you could have imagined. By practicing forgiveness in advance, you will be ready to use it when necessary. Ultimately I hope you will become a forgiving lover who can accept your partner's imperfections and refuse to take offense at your partner's behavior.

This book will teach you how to change the way you react to relationship problems so that you no longer feel upset and unbalanced for long periods after an argument or betrayal. If you approach your relationship with the understanding that things will sometimes go wrong and that you are ready with forgiveness, you will become a more powerful partner. As you forgive, you begin to reframe the way you discuss your relationship. You will find yourself telling stories of heroic understanding and unruffled self-acceptance instead of stories of grief and resentment.

Samantha and her husband had had a terrible car accident. She had found out that he was having an affair, and she was already angry because of his inability to hold a job. As they argued, her husband had lost control of their car and driven them into a tree. When Samantha was able to forgive her husband for their car accident and for the resulting chronic pain and medical bills, she realized that she could forgive anything. Moreover, if she could forgive anything, then why bother with getting upset in the first place? That is the fourth stage of forgiveness in action. That is the full power of forgiveness, and it will transform your life and your home.

I am not telling you to become passive or to simply forgive your partner and never offer a critical comment. I want to end this chapter with a story to remind you to take good care of yourself. Forgiveness is a great way to maintain your relationship and to care for yourself, but it is not the only way. Even if you forgive everyone in your family, you still have to deal with difficult individuals and painful situations.

A long time ago, a saint lived near a village. One day the saint was walking in the hills and came upon a rattlesnake lying in the grass. The snake lunged with its fangs bared, as if to bite the holy man. The saint smiled, and the snake was stopped by his kindness and love. The saint spoke to the rattler and asked the snake to give up biting the village's children. He said that in that way the snake would be better liked and cause less harm.

Because of the power the holy man possessed, the snake agreed to stop biting. The next week the saint was walking by the same spot and saw the snake on the ground lying in a pool of its own blood. The snake used what little strength it had to admonish the saint for almost killing him. "Look what happened to me when I took your advice. I am a bloody mess. Look what happened to me when I tried to be nice. Everyone is trying to hurt me." The saint looked at the snake, smiled, and said, "I never told you not to hiss."

FIVE

Step 1:
Dance with the One You Brought

The goal of this book is to teach you to forgive so that you can continue to experience a growing love for your partner. When we finally stop resenting the person we live with, we almost inevitably find that love blossoms in our lives. Happiness will grow in your relationship as forgiveness replaces resentment. The less resentment you hold toward your partner, the more love you will experience. The cost to your relationship in diminished love and happiness is the same whether you resent your partner for snoring or for leaving the toilet seat up. You will experience the same problems whether you resent your partner for something he or she did yesterday or for something from five years ago. The cost is always a diminished love in your heart and a greater hurt in your partner's. We pay a huge cost when we do not know how to forgive. When I teach forgiveness, I use seven steps to take students from resentment and frustration to a successful relationship.

There are many kinds of love we can develop in our lives—with friends, with siblings, with parents. But choosing to make love blossom with one person in a committed romantic relationship is a singular and worthy goal. It is a powerful thing for two people with different histories and struggles to commit to help and love each other in a sexually exclusive manner. This kind of relationship embodies a powerful opportunity to both give and receive love. It's like a scientific experiment: When we begin, we do not know the outcome, and we have no crystal ball to tell us. But we have a theory as to what will work or what won't work, and then we do the experiment to see if we are right. That experiment is our ongoing attempt to create a strong and satisfying relationship with our lover.

One reason lasting love can be difficult is that our theories of what will work are often wrong. Many of us come from homes where our parents did a poor job of getting along. They quarreled often or badly. They cheated on each other or committed other destructive acts. When they were together, they may have been defensive or withdrawn. As children, we observed their behavior and assumed it was normal. We watched and learned from them, and now we find ourselves acting in the same way. It can often be very difficult just to figure out how to deal with them as parents. When we grow up and enter into adult relationships, we use the patterns of behavior we learned at home and then wonder why things end up badly. Many adults don't know how to change, even when they find themselves acting in ways that do not support their marriage. The problem is that we rarely stop to examine whether the relationship patterns we use are the kind that can build a successful partnership.

One side of relationships that many of us observed growing up was resentment. We might have seen resentment in the form of criticism, harsh judgment, unkind speech, snide comments, scorn, a lack of support, or a sense that someone had been ripped off. These patterns are common in most families and leave their mark on each of us. Resentment is so common in relationships that most of us will have experienced it with our parents at some point. Of course, resentment rarely improves relationships and never makes our hearts more open. At some point, we experiment with resentment to deal with disappointment or unkindness, but failed marriages can get stuck in a pattern of resentment. In fact, scientific studies have shown that contempt is the hallmark of a relationship that is crashing and burning. It is a rare person who is honest enough to stop a failed experiment, and because of that, resentment rages on in many relationships.

Even though we logically know that our resentment isn't helping, it is hard to let go of the emotion. We focus on the problems we see in our lovers so that we do not have to stop being hostile and reevaluate how we communicate with them. Jennifer's boyfriend Keith was difficult and started many arguments with her; as a result, resentment became a normal part of her love life. In this kind of situation, our suffering overwhelms our good sense, and we take out our pain on the people we love. People who don't know how to forgive think that being resentful is a normal state to be in. The antidote to resentment is forgiveness through the use of these seven steps. With forgiveness we release the constriction we have placed on our hearts and love our partners for exactly who they are.

The first of the seven steps is the simplest, and for a few lucky people it can be the only step they need to take to release their grudges. There is a simple bottom line to this first step: the man or woman walking beside you is there for one simple reason—out of all the people out there, you chose this person as your partner, faults and all. You chose to join with this person and try to make a life together. The fact that your partner is with you only because you made a decision to invite him or her to join you is the simplest reason to be more forgiving of this person. Your decision to choose this partner also implies that you continue to be able to choose how much effort you will make toward sustaining a loving relationship with him or her. It is your positive exercise of choice that will be at the heart of a successful long-term relationship.

Do not allow your resentments to gloss over the fact that you made a decision to be your partner's lover. When you made that decision, you also agreed to let your partner love you. The problem that couples struggle with after this point is the question of how much responsibility we have for the quality of our relationship as it progresses. Sophie may have been wildly in love with Bill when they married in 1990, but does that mean she still has to treat him lovingly in 2006? What we need to ask ourselves is this: how much did I commit to behaving well after I chose my mate? Do I blame my partner if things turn out differently than we planned, or do I accept that risks and challenges are at the heart of all love relationships? Forgiveness allows you to continue to be kind and to honor your choice even when your partner's conduct has been poor. It allows you to love your partner in ways that accept his or her flawed humanness. Continuing to accept that we made a choice when we picked our lover is an ongoing affirmation that is essential in creating a successful relationship.

Before becoming a forgiveness teacher, I was a couples therapist. I worked with people like Rick and Arlene, who'd come into my office and scream at each other. Rick's words dripped with bitterness, and Arlene was full of contempt for her husband. Each hurled insults at the other and told me stories of grievance and disappointment in their relationship. Rick scowled as he told me how hard he tried to get Arlene to stop her lying. Arlene in turn could hardly listen before she jumped in with her harsh complaints about how annoying Rick and his constant criticisms were. I remember thinking that if this was how Rick and Arlene each treated the person they'd pledged their lives to, the one they'd promised to love and honor, then the rest of their social world better duck. Frankly, I thought they should be embarrassed to treat each other in that way.

Many couples speak and act in truly ugly ways toward each other. Why do people allow themselves to be so harsh with their best friend and the person they chose to love? In all my time as a couple's therapist, I never heard anyone utter this simple idea: *I willingly made a choice to be your lover, and now that it appears that decision did not work the way I hoped, what can I do to best honor my choice now?* Acknowledging this doesn't guarantee that you can fix your relationship, but it does remind you that you made a choice to be with your lover. When I worked with Arlene, I never saw her take ownership of her choice of Rick. Instead, I saw a lot of disgust for what she now saw as a lousy decision and contempt for how Rick had lied about who he was.

I see so much blame and hostility when I practice therapy or teach forgiveness classes. There is outright hostility, such as when Rick told Arlene that she was a bitch, but sometimes the blame is more subtle, as when Arlene told Rick that she felt sorry for him since he had done such a bad job of being a husband. I also see a lack of personal responsibility from both partners, such as when Arlene and Rick blamed each other for their own unkind and nasty behavior. Finally, I see a sense of entitlement—the belief that somehow we are owed great love without having to give it in return. I still wonder who put the gun to Rick's and Arlene's heads and the heads of all the distressed couples out there to force them to the altar or the bedroom.

The most accurate description of a successful marriage is one I read about in an interview with a nun. She was asked whether or not she considered her thirty years in the convent to have been a good life. She said that when she chose to become a nun, she also chose everything that happened to her after making that decision. She knew she could always leave the convent, but she believed that her original decision included what happened in the ensuing years. In her mind, she had made a decision to marry Jesus Christ, and it was a lifetime commitment that included any problems that went along with the decision; those problems were part of the package. While most of us choose people with more flaws than Jesus, the issue is the same. When we make a decision to choose Jerry or Sam, we are also choosing who Jerry or Sam is five or ten or twenty years from now.

According to the triangle theory of love discussed in chapter 1, the three sides of a relationship—passion, friendship, and commitment—need to be equally strong. Passion provides the spark that starts the relationship, while friendship allows for day-to-day communication and give-and-take. Commitment is the willingness to stick with the relationship over the years. Commitment also serves as a "safe space" for the more volatile aspects of the relationship. By itself, commitment—our promise to continue to honor the decision made many years ago—does not guarantee success in a relationship, but without it the offering of passion and friendship is wasted.

Let's look back for a moment at how you ended up with the partner you have. First you decided that you would rather be with someone than be alone. At that point you didn't have a specific person in mind, just the urge to find someone. As we get absorbed in the drama of our relationships, we tend to forget that this choice is the first critical play in the game of love. No one ever puts a gun to our heads and says, "Find a lover or I will blow your brains out." We make that choice to look for a partner rather than be alone. All our subsequent decisions emerge from this first one.

From that choice, you initiated action. You went out and met people and began the search for a good partner. Once you found someone interesting, you made the decision to spend time with that person to see whether the two of you were compatible. You chatted on the phone or hung out together a couple of times. After a few dates, you realized that you found aspects of this person attractive, and the feeling seemed to be mutual. Ralph and Arlene started dating when they were each in their early thirties. They both loved to do things like go to the beach, and they had a lot of fun together. Each of them did an emotional balance sheet on the other and decided that the good outweighed the bad. We all do this—anyone who has been in a relationship has tallied up their partner's good and bad points. When the audit reveals more good than bad, we stay together. When the bad outweighs the good, we end the relationship.

Robin and I explored this idea together in forgiveness training. She had come to the class because her ex-husband, Greg, was not making child support payments after their divorce. Robin had initiated the separation, even while Greg wished to remain married. Nonetheless, when the money did not come in as the court had ordered, she was angry. I asked her how she ended up married to Greg. Robin said that on their first date she liked Greg's sense of humor and his intelligence and so decided to spend more time with him. She also thought he was cute. After a few more dates, she continued to be drawn to him.

After this initial phase went well, Robin and Greg did what most people do: they decided to try out being part of a twosome rather than remaining two solo-flyers. They became an exclusive couple after about four months of dating. She said the decision to do so was mutual, and she made her choice because the "relationship had potential." She really liked the way Greg treated her, she appreciated his values, and she loved his sense of humor. Like most couples, Robin and Greg had only nice things to say about each other at this stage of their relationship—in their minds the good outweighed the bad.

Soon afterward Robin became pregnant. Abortion was not an option, since Robin did not believe in it. Both she and Greg had "been around the block," and so they hastily decided to get married. However, Robin admitted, she would not have married Greg as speedily if she had not been pregnant. She said this as if her unplanned pregnancy made her decision to marry less binding, or as if she was somehow less responsible for her choice. As we continued to talk, Robin implied that being older and unwilling to try with someone else were not legitimate reasons to choose Greg. Although Greg was less inclined to marry, he decided to go along with Robin's decision. Both chose the other thinking that the decision to become a couple was a better choice than the decision not to. They did an inner balance sheet and saw more benefit in staying together than in separating. Clearly, their decision was not made under perfect circumstances, but it was a decision nonetheless.

Clients like Robin and Greg have shown me how often our partnering decisions are made under difficult or stressful circumstances. Sometimes we make these choices without the time or information we would usually need to make such an important decision. Robin and Greg's situation is pretty common. Some people marry hastily because one of them is about to be deployed in the armed forces. Sometimes there is pressure to rush a decision because one partner is ill or rebounding from a bad relationship. And of course, when there are difficult stepchildren involved whose needs must be considered, the decision is never easy. Choosing a partner is rarely a neat and tidy process, but it is a choice nonetheless. Whether we make our decision in easy or difficult circumstances, we can't deny that we weighed different factors before making it.

What I am getting at is this: no one forced Robin or Greg to go through their process of choice and commitment, and no one forced you or me either. Making a choice does not guarantee that the choice will always be ideal or that there won't be regrets. The important point here is that, out of the six billion people on this planet, you picked the person you wanted as your lover. You did not choose her sister or the attractive contestant on the TV game show. You used the available information and your decision-making capability to choose Sally or Dave or John, with all that person's possible problems and failings. You chose your lover using free will and made the best decision you could with the information you had. That is the essence of what it means to make a choice—you make the best decision you can with the information you have available. When we choose our mate, we select one specific person with whom to try to do our absolute best. We promise that person that we will try to be as kind and loving as possible, and that we will practice loyalty and offer solace as needed. We also promise to forgive our partner when we can for his or her flaws, weaknesses, silly habits, or selfishness.

To forgive, you need to understand that everything that has happened in your relationship came about because of your willing decision to join with your partner. Just like the nun, your choice included everything that came after that commitment. In this forgiveness step, you take responsibility for your decision, and once you do that, there is no one to blame when things go wrong. Relationships do fail, and things can go wrong. Sometimes we enter into a relationship but are not skilled enough to pull it off. Robin chose Greg. Ideally, she would have preferred to not be pressured by her pregnancy into rushing a decision, but she had chosen to have sex with Greg. Without that decision, there would have been no pregnancy.

Be honest with yourself. Accept the decisions you made to grow your relationship and realize the difference it makes when you own your part in the process.

Accepting responsibility for the fact that you chose your part-ner does not make your life easy. Nor does it commit you to staying with your partner. But if you accept responsibility for your decision, then you continue to have a choice in your behav-ior, attitudes, speech, and thoughts about your partner because it was your decision. If you blame your partner, you are forgetting why you are in the position to blame him or her. You chose to be with this person. If you are dissatisfied, you are forgetting why you are in the position of being dissatisfied with him or her. You can choose to forgive your partner for being the person he or she is, or you can resent your partner and feel sorry for yourself.

Think of your relationship as a scary but exciting ride at an amusement park. After much prompting, you decide to try it out. You've heard your friends screaming as they go around the track, and frankly you have doubts about whether this experience is for you. When you finally decide to get on the ride, it's prob-ably for some silly reason, like showing off to your friends. Whatever your reasons, you are making a personal choice to be on the ride. That decision doesn't guarantee a smooth ride. In fact, it's likely to be bumpy and even terrifying in places. So too with your relationship. The fact that you chose each other makes it no one's fault if things are difficult or don't work out exactly as planned.

When I began working with Samantha and Jesse, they had been married for eight years. They had two children and owned a business together. Things had not been easy during their life together. Jesse had been sick, and Samantha had lost both of her parents in a horrible accident. I asked them how they had coped, and they both replied that their secret was commitment. They had both made a choice to be with each other, and they were going to honor that choice as best they could. To them honoring their choice meant accepting their life and doing their best. Both

Samantha and Jesse realized that their struggle was with areas of
the life they had created together, not with each other. No matter
how bad things got, each of them always made the effort to let
the other know they cared.

Three inconvenient truths make this simple and obvious step
to forgiveness challenging. The first truth is that every relationship is a risk. The second truth is that each and every relationship will end. And the third truth is that we can neither change
nor control our partner's actions. All three truths point to the
same message: when we commit to someone, we don't know
what we will get or how long it will last. Because of these three
truths, every relationship will have challenges and be difficult at
times. We can't choose whether or not to have difficult experiences—all we can do is choose who to have those difficult experiences with.

The only certainty is that our relationship will end, with either
death or dissolution. This truth is profoundly difficult to accept
because it shows just how painful any relationship can be. We
may like to think that we are choosing someone for eternity, but
in fact our love can last only until death do us part, or earlier.
People suffer hugely when they do not acknowledge the uncertainties at the heart of any relationship. When you say, "I do,"
you are choosing who you will experience these uncertainties
and vulnerabilities with, not making a choice as to whether or
not they will happen. When you set up a life with someone, you
are in part agreeing to experience the pains and difficulties of life
with them.

In the medical world, a surgeon is required to get informed
consent from a patient before operating. The patient must fully
understand the risks of the procedure beforehand and agree to go
ahead with it. When Frank agreed to have open-heart surgery, he
knew that the procedure might cause blood clots. Sarah knew

that her cosmetic surgery could cause scarring. Each person chooses the hope of a good result with the understanding that problems are possible. I tell people to have the same attitude toward their relationships. We enter into our partnerships and assume the risks whether we sign an informed consent contract or not. When people are in the glow of infatuation and new love, they rarely think about the risks they assume when they choose their partner.

When we first start to date someone, we don't know the personal details about that person, nor do we know what will happen in the future. Every relationship carries a risk because our ability to know another person is limited and we have no idea what our future will hold together. When we commit, we commit to a promise and not a certainty. We offer our partner our promise to love him or her, and we have to hope our partner offers the same in return. There is no guarantee that our relationship will work; all we can do is commit to do our best within these significant limitations. Our relationship with our partner is an experiment. We do what we can to improve it and give it the best chance of success.

Any new relationship carries the risk that our lover might be unkind to us down the road. At the beginning of our relationship, we don't know how our partner will respond to the stress of parenthood or the difficulties of a terrible boss. We know there is a chance our partner could choose to be with someone else. Our relationship could be damaged by illness or religious differences, or our loved one could simply fall out of love. We have to deal with the possibility that our children could be born disabled or that we might never be able to have children at all. There will certainly be change in the relationship—there is just no way of knowing whether it will be for better or worse.

I hear so many stories of couples who accepted these risks

only to see them realized. The fact that these kinds of stories are so common shows just how tremendous the uncertainty is in any relationship and how willingly people blind themselves to the risks. My clients tell me many stories about how their lover disappointed them. What I don't hear very often is any acknowledgment of informed consent—the admission that they made a choice and therefore assumed the risks. Something like: "I knew there would be things that would go wrong but chose to go ahead anyway." Mary could complain all she wanted about how her boyfriend mistreated her, but she needed to acknowledge that she was aware of the risk of this when her relationship began. Laura told me that she was shocked to discover that her husband Sheldon didn't want children, but she didn't acknowledge that that was the risk she took when she married him. People can change, yet when Frank was dumped by his wife after four years of marriage, he was unable to understand that some change is inevitable. Jim felt that his wife was a slob and he was angry that she refused to cook, but he was unable to accept that even the best partner has some difficult traits.

Assuming some risks and accepting that relationships can be difficult does not mean we have to stay and be brutalized in a bad situation. A husband does not need to stay with a cheating wife. Sally chose to marry a man who ended up having violent tendencies, but she was not required to stay and be abused. Sally would have done well, however, to acknowledge that she made an error in her choice of mate and that her relationship experiment was a failure. Looking at it that way would have created a lot less hostility and self-pity. When we accept that we chose our partner, there is no one to blame when the choice does not work out. We can choose to get into a relationship, and we can also choose to get out. Until we make that choice to leave, it is our choice to stay.

The flip side to all of this is sometimes fantastic: choosing to take on the risks of a relationship might also show you that your partner is even better than you could have imagined. The trying situations that destroy some relationships could strengthen yours. One of my clients, Sandy, never knew how wonderful her husband Sunny was until her father fell ill. Sunny spent days on end at the hospital, taking care of her dad. She did not know the depth of care her husband was capable of until he was challenged. John was awed at his wife Pam's ability as a parent. Pam had grown up in a broken home and had poor relationships with both of her parents. John was very concerned that he would have to handle all the parenting duties with their baby. However, Pam was ready, willing, and able when their first child was born. John was awed as his wife handled the stresses of new motherhood with aplomb.

When we choose a partner, there is no guarantee that we have picked the best person with whom to conduct a lifelong experiment in love. But by its very nature, risk can go both ways. Besides discovering that the person we chose can be a great parent or a wonderful caretaker, it's quite possible that he or she will turn out to be loving enough to heal some of the wounds we carry from childhood, or strong enough to keep the family intact if we get sick. It's also quite possible that together we may be better than we are on our own.

Robin and Greg had four kids together, but I was dumbstruck to hear how dubious she had been about Greg from the beginning. Robin had been overwhelmed by doubts as her first pregnancy proceeded. If she was so uncertain then, why did she go ahead and have another three children with Greg? Once she had the kids, why did she then blame him for the failure of their relationship? I thought this was ridiculous, and said so. Needless to say, Robin was not pleased to hear my assessment. Like many other unhappy spouses, she found it easier to blame her partner than to accept that she simply chose to participate in an unsuccessful relationship experiment again and again. Like every other person in a love affair, she had chosen to be there, from the day it began until the day it ended.

The scariest risk in a relationship is the uncertainty over how and when it will end. We have informed consent—we know the relationship will end one day—but we don't know when or how. The end of a love affair is so painful, and causes so much anxiety, that most of us would rather be surprised when it happens than deal with the risk head on. People in the glow of young love do not accept that their relationship will be over one day. People with kids find it difficult to see the temporary nature of their children's youth or to contemplate that their children will become old men and women one day. Yet no relationship lasts forever, and either death or a desire to quit will end every affair. When a love affair ends, we feel the same vulnerability and anxiety that we do when we fall in love. The only promise we can make when we choose our partners is that we will love them as long as we can.

Once we accept the temporary nature of a relationship, we are able to understand the nature of our choice to love. It is a choice that asks a lot of us, and the truth is that we have a limited window of opportunity when we can really give ourselves to another. Our partner also has a short time in which to give himself or herself to us. As scary as it is to contemplate, the reality is that neither of us knows when that window of opportunity will close. Our relationship will end one day, and all we will be left with are the consequences of our choices. When we make the decision to stay with our partner or leave, we are making a temporary choice. We will be separated from our lover one day, either deliberately through divorce or disinterest or involuntarily through death. Our partner faces the same reality.

Accepting that our relationship is temporary also carries the realization that our decision to make it work is one we make over and over every day. Our offer of love is not good forever, and how can we ask ourselves what we will do next week when there is no certainty that our relationship has a next week? Our lover could leave us at any minute, so surely we should be on our best behavior at all times? If we choose not to be, that is our choice. When we understand that our lover is choosing to be with us—exercising the same freedom to do so that we have—we can see the beauty of that decision, both our lover's choice to be with us and vice versa. This realization helps us to not take our partner for granted.

Relationships end every day, for numerous reasons. Joan and Herb married late in life. It was a second marriage for both, and they spent three fantastic years together before Herb died at sixty-one. Linda's lover left her after four years of living together. Their relationship was longer than Joan and Herb's, but Linda still felt cheated because Alex left by choice, not because of death. Alice was devastated when her lover decided he did not want to move in with her and ended their eighteen-month relationship. Jack and Mary divorced after nineteen years of marriage. Their kids had grown up and left home, and they did not have enough passion to stay together. John and Marilyn died together in a car crash after forty-seven years of marriage. Each of these relationships ended differently, but all ended earlier than at least one of the partners would have wished.

I hope that you honor the choice you have made with your partner. Accepting the fact that you made a decision to pick your loved one stops you from harboring resentment and helps you to love your partner as much as possible. Time is short and precious, so don't waste any of it in blaming yourself or your partner. It may be that you made your decision to marry hastily or without all the information you needed. Perhaps you underestimated parts of your lover's pain or overestimated your ability to deal with it. You can't know how things will turn out in the future; all you really know is the name of the person you chose to share an unpredictable life with. You can't predict the variables that will affect your relationship. Even if you could, you don't know how you and your partner will change over time. Be gentle with yourself and your lover: we fall in love with certain people for a reason, so we shouldn't be angry when they are just being themselves.

The truly difficult, gritty part of a relationship comes when our loved one shows traits that bother us but that they refuse to change. At some point everyone displays qualities that their partner doesn't like or acts in ways that are destructive to the relationship, and as discussed already, one of the most difficult aspects of any relationship is recognizing that our partner does not always do what we want him or her to do. But it is human nature for all of us to put our own needs first. That's a duh. All lovers bring their problematic behaviors with them into a relationship. The only thing either partner has control over is deciding which of the other's annoying qualities to deal with.

By mentally signing an informed consent form saying, "I know my partner will do things I do not like or understand," we acknowledge that the future is unpredictable and that relationships are temporary. The simple truth is that human nature is selfish: our lovers are likely to try to satisfy their own desires and wishes more than ours. When we decide to stay with our partners, we are also choosing to stay with their flaws, be they Jack's sloppiness or Stan's laziness or Arlene's lack of responsibility. As long as you choose to stay in the relationship, you need to bring a willingness to forgive to the mix. By choosing a particular person at a particular time, you are also choosing the particular experiences he or she brings to the relationship. Every rosebush comes with thorns; if you do not like thorns, you might want to choose to plant a different kind of flower. If you only want to be involved in relationships that you are able to control, then you should think seriously of getting a house full of pets instead of a lover.

Another reality for which you need to give informed consent is the virtual certainty that your lover will not love you exactly the way you want to be loved. You want a white rose, but he shows up with a red rose and a big smile on his face saying, "Aren't red roses gorgeous?" Sandy desperately wanted more romance from her husband Gary. He in turn wanted to spend every weekend with his wife engaged in active pursuits and fun activities. His picture of a perfect wife did not include an interest in flowers and poetry and bad novels. Sandy's idea of a successful relationship centered on having more time with Gary talking and sharing closeness. Sandy and Gary were lucky in that they had a strong marriage, and over time each accepted the fact that the other was not the same as the person they had pictured in their heads in the beginning. Both Sandy and Gary offered the love they were able to offer, and both were wise enough to forgive the color of the offered rose. Neither of them was happy until they accepted their choice of mate, grieved the loss of their idealized partner, and thereby forgave each other.

Here's the deal. The next time you are frustrated because your partner is being himself or herself, ask yourself, "Why am I here?" The answer will be something like: "I chose to try to make it work with him/her. I selected this person because I believed he/she offered me the best chance of a satisfying relationship. My partner selected me for the same reason. If that is no longer true, there is no one to blame because the experiment failed." If, on the other hand, it is still true that your partner offers you the best chance of a satisfying relationship, you need to forgive both yourself and your partner so that you can keep a clear head and an open heart. Once you've done that, work hard to make your relationship work. Let go, love as best you can, and join your lover in creating your future.

SIX

Step 2:
Recognize That Everyone Is
Flawed ... Including You

Okay, so you understand that you chose to be with your partner. You realize that you could have decided to go it alone, but you did not. Clearly, your relationship will end at some point, and your loved one won't always do what you want. Now that you've accepted the concept of choice in a relationship, you are probably wondering what else I have to offer. While choice is the foundation of forgiveness, it is by no means all there is. The next step in this process is to honor without resentment the flawed nature of the human being with whom you share your life. By definition, you are with someone who has significant limitations. Unfortunately, you did not get in the line where they were offering saints, angels, personal saviors, or slaves. You got in the line for a regular person, warts and all. Learning to accept your partner's limitations with tenderness is the next step of forgiveness and the opening to a true love.

One of the inescapable problems of being part of a couple is that you need two people involved. Problems emerge the minute another person enters your orbit. Your new partner is bound to have significant differences from you. He will be interested in things that bore you and will have habits that you find disagreeable. She might love pizza, but hates Italian food. Perhaps you live for hockey, but she is bored to tears by sports. Or you like quiet and he wants the TV on all the time. Your partner has had experiences unlike yours. He was raised differently than you, went to a different school, has had his own unique family experiences, and probably works in a different field. Like most people, your partner probably thinks her way of living is the right way, and she insists that she is right and you are wrong.

Even if you have the most perfect partner imaginable, there are going to be plenty of things to disagree about. This is true even before one or both of you do something wrong. You know you will disagree about things even before the cheating, the lying, the business failures, or the bad parenting. Friction and arguments are inevitable in relationships because of our differences; we fight when we don't share opinions, upbringings, habits, or experiences. It is important to argue well about our differences. Not arguing or arguing poorly can actually be worse than a good disagreement. In a healthy couple, each forgives the other for being different and even for being themselves. To do this we need to communicate well and on a regular and ongoing basis.

No matter who you pick as a life partner, there are guaranteed to be differences between you. Human beings are an interesting species, and everyone has their quirks. Not only do we like things a certain way, but sometimes we can be fanatical about having things the way we want them. John had always eaten his salad before his main dish, and he knew that was the right way to do it. His girlfriend believed that the salad should come after the entrée. John thought his girlfriend was nuts for serving salad the way she did, and insensitive for not putting his needs first.

Sally was a wallflower, and her husband Sid loved being the center of attention. Both of them thought their way of interacting at parties was better, and they had made their ideas on this minor issue a problem in their relationship. Both of these couples elevated minor differences into bigger issues when they fought. Most couples will blow small issues up until they think they are worth fighting over.

The second point is that everybody makes mistakes. John would promise his wife Laura that he would pick up the dry cleaning and then forget to do so for an entire week. She would remind him every day after work, and he'd still forget. For her part, Laura regularly forgot to get the car washed and never got the oil changed. One time their car died in rush-hour traffic because the engine was down three quarts of oil.

John misplaced things that he did not want to do, such as his taxes, and they were audited as a result of his laziness. Laura forgot to pick up his parents at the airport, and they were stranded there until John got a tense phone call at work asking if there had been an accident.

Couples face more general mistakes on a day-to-day basis. For instance, does anyone really know the best way to raise a child? How do we teach and discipline them so that they turn out well? Even the best parents are going to make mistakes as they try to figure this out. Do any of us really know the best way to talk to our lovers? How on earth do we comfort them when they are scared, or console them when their parents die? What's the best way to help them when they have problems with their own families? We try our best, but some failure is inevitable. Your partner will not succeed all the time, so your job is to gently forgive his or her flaws. To forgive is to accept your partner's poor judgment or laziness without prejudice. To forgive is to accept the limitations that your lover brings to the party.

Third, our partners act in selfish ways that cause us pain at times. They get caught up in their own desires and do things that affect us negatively. When Denise got the urge to spend money, she bought a huge TV that she and her boyfriend couldn't afford. Likewise, Sarah insisted on hiring a babysitter two nights a week so that she could go out with her friends, even though it was too expensive. How about Frank, who blew off visiting his in-laws to go fishing? Or Jackson, who tore his cartilage playing baseball with a damaged knee and missed another week of work? Take Betty, who drove Gordon crazy with her demands for sex when he was tired from caring for their young kids and working all the time. Each of these people did what they did because they felt like it. They did not mean to do their partner harm. They actually didn't think about how their actions or demands affected their partner. They were focused on their own desires and did not think about the consequences of their actions.

These are examples of generally benign acts with modest consequences. None of the people involved acted with deliberately malicious intent or caused long-term harm. By contrast, some people are endangered by lovers who commit acts of cruelty that are extensions of their everyday failures, selfishness, or quirks. Families are wrecked every day by parents who abuse drugs or alcohol. Some people live with physically or emotionally abusive lovers who hit them or force them to have sex against their will. Selfishness will cause people to commit adultery, steal money, and use violence. These destructive behaviors are the lethal versions of the more common and less harmful acts of indifference, failure, and selfishness that we all experience.

When you add your flaws to those of your partner, you start to realize just how challenging it can be to get along. It is human nature to focus on your partner's mistakes and flaws and minimize your own. Very early in my career, I worked with Ted and

Irene. Ted started the first session by listing all of Irene's flaws in obsessive detail. He described how she could be a better lover, better cook, and more attentive partner. Not only that, but Irene also needed to earn more money, be less resistant to change, and appreciate how patient he was with her. Ted spent fifteen minutes telling me all the ways in which his wife needed a makeover. It was like an auto mechanic's detailed itemization of the repairs needed on the family car. Irene deserved combat pay for putting up with this guy. After about fifteen minutes, Ted stopped in his tracks and simply looked at me. I had no idea how to respond, since I was very new to therapy and they were the first couple I had ever seen. After what seemed like ten minutes, I figured out what to say.

I told Ted that I appreciated that there were a number of things he wanted to improve in their marriage. His openness was a good start to therapy, and it was important that he trust me enough to be frank. I ran down his list of complaints and then asked him this question. "If Irene became a sex goddess who could cook like Julia Child, make a lot of money, was easy to talk to, and gave you her undivided attention, she would be a pretty special individual. What would a super woman like that possibly want with you?" Ted was stunned by my question and tried to stammer out a response. Irene was laughing hysterically, practically crying, telling me, "This is how I tolerate Ted!" Irene was very wise; she knew that she and Ted were both regular people, and that one of Ted's bad traits was criticism. She had her own weaknesses, and that was the way things were. Ted was so busy cataloging Irene's weaknesses that he missed both his own flaws and the phenomenal love and patience Irene showed him on a regular basis. I wanted Ted to see the amazing love he was so busy criticizing and realize that he had plenty of bad traits of his own.

If you want to relate honestly with your lover, you need to pay attention to the annoying difficulties you bring to the relationship. We all do things that would stress Mother Teresa's patience at times. You might not be a great bargain yourself. You have quirks you will go to the mat with that are probably nothing more than idiosyncratic preferences. You make poor decisions because you are in a rush or do not have enough information and may not be able to acknowledge that you made a mistake. Everybody is occasionally selfish enough to damage their relationships. Perhaps you put your own well-being over that of your significant other. Maybe you are too sensitive to your lover's speech and react with hurt. There may be times when you are cool to your partner for not giving you the level of affection you need. In each case, you are prioritizing your needs over the relationship's needs. None of these kinds of behaviors are necessarily lethal to a relationship, but they can weaken it eventually.

Every one of us has come home tired from a hard day at work and ignored the more pressing needs of our partner or children. Sometimes your lover is more tired or more in need than you are. However, you may not always see your partner's need, even when it is right in front of you, because in your exhaustion you have nothing left to give him or her. If you ever think that you are flawless, try this exercise. Ask your partner to tell you anything you did today that was difficult or caused your partner stress. Have your partner write down a list of things that he or she regularly has to forgive you for if the relationship is going to thrive. If you ask sincerely, you will get honest answers, and if you are lucky, the relationship will be strengthened with more humility and forgiveness.

I'm not sharing this list of relationship problems to get you to renounce love and join a monastery. I am trying to remind you to be humble about your own flaws and to remember that you too regularly require forgiveness. If you want a successful relationship, you need to be gentle with the inevitable flaws of your lover. I also want you to understand that dealing kindly with the mistakes and wounds of your partner is how you open yourself up to true love. It would be easy to get along with Ted's ideal mate. Coming home to a passionate sex partner who was also a great cook, hard worker, high wage earner, good communicator, and all-around fabulous person would be great. The problem with that scenario is twofold. First, what would such a perfect person want with us, and second, how would we learn to really love if our needs were always met with a smile? It is easy to love those who never test us because they are always giving and never in a bad mood. It is difficult to love real people because they ask us to give and give and forgive and be humble.

Ted's ideal doesn't exist, so there must be something we need to learn from our partners' weaknesses and our own weaknesses. It may be that when we love our partners in a way that includes their differences and flaws, we go deep enough to create an enduring partnership. When we are cruel and dismissive about our differences and our partners' weaknesses, we impose our fantasy of how a lover should be on a live human being. We try to get Sarah to be more talkative than she is, or think we can talk Josie into being less nervous than she actually is. We've all been rejected, and we all know how painful it can be. Every time we impose our demands on our partners, we tell them that we don't love them the way they are. Our actions hurt our partners and show them that we have a lot of work to do to become better lovers ourselves. Forgiveness emerges once we accept the challenge of loving the real person we are with. Only then can we begin to develop a deep and lasting partnership.

You still need to be open with your partner about the things he or she does that are hurtful, offensive, or selfish. You don't have to be a martyr about it. A strong, healthy relationship needs open communication, and letting your partner know how he or she is hurting the relationship is necessary for things to improve. The important thing is to forgive your lover before you initiate that talk. Then you can talk openly and pleasantly, without anger. Practice stage four forgiveness so that there is no bitterness when you have your conversation. Keep in mind that conflicts don't really change over the course of a relationship. Seventy percent of the conflicts that were there at the start of your relationship will remain in place until the end, so keep your expectations within reason.

Sexual incompatibility is a normal problem that can lead to significant distress if handled badly. The problem starts when one partner wants more sex than the other, and both are willing to fight about it rather than compromise. Betty was a highly sexed woman married to Gordon, a man with only a modest sex drive. Before they had kids, Betty and Gordon had been able to work things out satisfactorily. However, life became more stressful and busy after the children were born, and Gordon became even less interested in sex. He was working full-time, then helping out at home. He simple didn't have any energy left for sex. The sexual incompatibility between Betty and Gordon made both of them angry.

Betty was mad because Gordon was frustrating her sex drive, which served as her stress reducer, and Gordon was mad because he was tired and always feeling pressured. The arguments about sex were not the biggest problem they faced. In truth, both partners had reasonable points of view. The main problem was that both Betty and Gordon felt that they were right and demanded that the other change. Thus, the way they handled their initial problem had spawned a second one. Now they had to worry about not only their sex drives but also the emotional distress they were putting on their relationship. The anger, stress, and self-pity that Betty and Gordon felt about the sexual frequency problem became the problem that consumed their marriage. Had they been able to forgive each other for their righteousness, stubbornness, and selfishness, they might have worked out the sexual frequency problem.

Forgiveness does not solve every problem. But it does reduce the intensity of emotional distress so that our problems can be talked about and solved if possible. Blaming our partners for not being the person we want them to be creates anger in both us and them. This anger causes stress. Every time Betty got angry with Gordon, she put a lot of stress in her body. Now when Betty thought about their sexual problems, her body released stress-related chemicals designed to prepare her for a dangerous situation. Her body went into a "fight-or-flight" response that obviously affected how she dealt with her husband.

The fight-or-flight response is triggered in large part by activation of the sympathetic nervous system, which is the branch of the autonomic nervous system whose goal is to rev your body up to protect you from danger. The autonomic nervous system controls inner organs such as the heart, as well as smooth muscles and breathing. Your autonomic nervous system has another branch called the parasympathetic system, which calms you down after the danger has passed. Both of these systems are operating all of the time. When a danger such as tired Gordon or demanding Betty comes into view, the sympathetic system gears up and controls the action.

Under the influence of these chemicals, Betty and Gordon had only two choices: fight or flight. These are poor choices, however, when you're trying to solve problems creatively or figure out a situation as emotionally charged as sex. The fight-or-flight response alters the brain's ability to think. The stress chemicals protect us from danger by limiting the amount of electrical activity available to the thinking part of the brain. This is the result of the blood flow changes mentioned earlier. When Gordon told Betty that he was so upset that he couldn't even think straight, he was telling the truth.

When Betty's body was prepped for danger, it didn't waste her mental resources on thinking through the situation. Her biology said that survival was most important. So, if danger was on the horizon in the form of a resistant Gordon, she couldn't be trusted to try to figure out a complex situation.

Betty's memories of Gordon's cruelty put her in fight-or-flight mode. Her body was literally trying to save her life by diverting some electrical energy from the thinking part of her brain to the more primitive and reactive parts of her brain. The problem for Betty was that her body was overreacting. Remembering Gordon's past unkindness was not a dangerous situation. The stress was wasted, and the relationship suffered. At any one of these moments, forgiveness would have been more helpful than anger. You do not need a fight-or-flight response when you tell your wife that you would like more help, sex, or love. You do not need sympathetic nervous system arousal to explain for the thirty-fifth time how unfair it was that your husband was not helpful when the baby was born. But your body can't tell the difference between a real or imagined problem and responds the only way it knows how.

The mistake all the Betty's and Gordon's make while under the influence of the stress chemicals is to blame their mental and physical distress on the person who hurt them. This mistake makes peace so much harder to find. Betty gave Gordon a huge amount of power over her by holding him responsible for her feelings. Because she was feeling hurt, she got upset every time she thought about Gordon's lack of caring. This thinking led her to feel like the victim of someone who was more powerful than she was. By blaming our body's normal protective stress response on the person who has hurt us, we make ourselves feel small and weak compared to their perceived power. Gordon also suffered: his futile anger made him feel helpless and disempowered. Gordon could have ended this futile cycle if he had understood the power of forgiveness.

Betty's anger at Gordon sent him a very clear message. Her actions were telling him that her love was conditional: she wanted Gordon, but a Gordon with a Betty sex drive. Of course, this would have been impossible. Now every time they discussed sex Betty started to have a stress reaction. Her blood flowed out from her thinking centers, and she was unable to think rationally and sensitively about her husband and their differing sexual needs and responses to stress. Like many other people in similar situations, they now had a second problem—managing their anger, pain, and despair. This second problem can quickly become more dangerous to a marriage than the original disagreement.

Forgiveness allows a couple to resolve the second problem so that they can realistically address the first one. To reach this second step to forgiveness you have to accept that your lover will be different than you are, may not want to change, and may even be annoying. Being forgiving means understanding that you can't force your lover to change just because you are uncomfortable, inconvenienced, or disturbed. It is up to you to manage your emotional reactions, not the responsibility of your partner. Once you are able to forgive, you can deal with the first problem with dignity and openness, not blame.

How do the differences, quirks, selfishness, and failures we bring to our relationships become grievances such as the ones afflicting Gordon and Betty? Why do normal tensions and episodic problems get blown up into relationship-crushing resentment?

Many relationships are troubled by unequal sex drives, but most survive it. There is nothing etched in stone that says sexual incompatibility has to create a major problem. Since the problem itself didn't have to lead to this kind of marital trouble, it must have been the way in which Betty and Gordon were dealing with it. I call the thinking process that leads to grievances like this "trying to enforce unenforceable rules."

This is when you try to control something it is not in your power to control. Betty could not control how often Gordon would have sex with her. She had no power over the institution of marriage or its requirement of monogamy. Have you ever tried to force your lover to do something he or she did not want to do? Have you ever tried to get what you needed from your wife when she was too busy? Have you ever demanded that your husband be nicer to you when he was not in the mood? Trying to force our lovers to give us something that they don't want to give is folly.

How often and how deeply we get upset with our lovers depends on the kinds of relationship rules we have set up. When you have too many unenforceable rules or try too hard to enforce workable rules, you create stress. When you try to enforce a rule that is under your control, your life goes smoothly. Remember: there are rules you can enforce and those that you cannot. When I tell my three-year-old child to stay out of my bedroom, I can put up a gate to keep her out. If she crawls over the gate, I can bring her back to the living room or I can put up a bigger gate. I can keep my child away from my bedroom if I have the will and energy to try. Generally I can make my three-year-old stay where I want.

On the other hand, you are setting yourself up for frustration if you insist that your husband be home by 10:30 every evening. You can make the rule and nag him about it all you want. However, your husband makes the ultimate decision about when he returns home. He could be late for a number of reasons: perhaps he got stuck in bad traffic, perhaps he decided to go out with his buddies and not you, or perhaps he just forgot what time he was supposed to be home. He may not care what you think. Demanding that your husband come home at a specific time is an unenforceable rule. You cannot physically control your forty-three-year-old spouse in the same way you can control your three-year-old child. Your spouse has a choice to obey you or not. Trying to force your husband to come home earlier than he wants to is like herding cats or asking the sun to rise in the west. You are trying to do something that goes against your husband's natural behavior, and you will be endlessly frustrated if you keep trying to do it.

Nearly all relationship problems begin when our partners break an unenforceable rule. Your frustrated attempt to enforce such a rule is at the root of your anger toward your loved one. Feelings of anger, helplessness, or depression are all indications that you are trying to enforce something that cannot be enforced. Your anger is telling you that things are not working out the way you want them to. These situations are painful because you are not able to control them, even though you try over and over to do so. When Betty and Gordon tried to force each other to bend to their desires, they were just frustrating themselves. Both could argue all they wanted that they were right, but the other person was still not going to change.

If most of your partner's actions cause you a good deal of emotional distress, you may be trying to enforce an unenforceable rule. We cling to our unenforceable rules and refuse to accept our partner's mistakes, flaws, and disagreeable traits, thinking that we should not have to put up with them. This is like clinging to the anchor of a ship you fell off of. As you gasp your last breath, you're still complaining that the anchor was there to keep you and your boat safe, and damn it, dragging you to the bottom of the sea isn't helping. The anchor is wrong. It hasn't read the anchor rulebook and doesn't know the right way to do its job.

Here is my simple definition of what constitutes a rule in your life: any expectation you have for how your partner or other people in your life should act, think, or feel. Having rules in a marriage is normal, and most of them are healthy rather than destructive. We all have rules for things like dressing appropriately, speaking correctly, or drinking within limits. We may have other rules about spending money wisely, raising children well, or obeying social laws like the "twelve-items-or-less" line at the supermarket. We probably also have rules for the way our lovers talk to us and the way our kids treat us.

To have an unenforceable rule is to maintain an expectation that you do not have the power to make happen. Perhaps you expect your lover to treat you as well as you treat him or her. Maybe you think your lover should have sex with you when you want, or should listen attentively every time you talk. You might expect to be told every day that you are beautiful, or perhaps you expect your partner to earn a certain amount of money.

When you try and fail to enforce one of your unenforceable rules, you become angry, bitter, despondent, and helpless. Trying to force something that you cannot control to go your way is an exercise in frustration. You can't force your spouse to love you or to stop cheating; nor can you force your kids to treat you respectfully. The more unenforceable rules you have, the more likely you are to feel agitated and disappointed with your marriage. When you cling to unenforceable rules, you leave yourself open to pain every time one of them is broken.

Bernice got upset each and every time Don was late getting home. She didn't like being left alone while he was out drinking.

It also made her angry that Don did not obey her rules; he wasn't doing what he was supposed to. Bernice's attempt to enforce several unenforceable rules was futile. Part of her anger was a legitimate response to Don's carelessness and destructive behavior. However, another part of her unhappiness came from trying to force Don to come home on time—she simply did not have the power to make him do so. Instead of accepting his lack of reliability, Bernice tried to maintain her illusion of control. Whenever Don violated her unenforceable rules, she became angry. It never occurred to Bernice to wonder whether the rules she had set for Don were realistic.

Bernice thought that Don should be home at a reasonable time and that he was wrong to abuse drugs. She also believed that Don should love her, be reliable, and show up to work on time. Bernice constructed a host of rules that Don brazenly broke time and time again. As Bernice struggled to force Don to obey the unenforceable rules she had created, she started to become emotionally disturbed. This second problem obscured the real problem of Don's poor behavior. I don't want to suggest that Don's behavior was acceptable, or that it is easy to live with a substance abuser. Bernice was going to be hurt dealing with the shambles of her marriage no matter how she handled it. However, I do think that by trying to enforce unenforceable rules, Bernice made things much harder for herself and lessened her ability to make the difficult decisions she needed to make.

Lucy was a single mom with two kids who was married to Mark for seventeen years. Even when they were together Lucy was a de facto single parent, since Mark worked all the time. They didn't get to spend much time together, and Mark never attended any of their children's school functions. Lucy was so fed up that she finally confronted Mark with her frustrations. After talking things through, they made a date to spend the next Saturday together. Bright and early on Saturday, Lucy found a note from Mark saying that he was going to the office for a few minutes. Mark was gone for the next four hours. Lucy was furious. When he finally did come home, she screamed and threw kitchen utensils at him. Mark could not understand why his wife got so upset. As far as he was concerned, he was just getting some work done, but in reality he had broken his wife's unenforceable rule for the last time.

A common example of an unenforceable rule is "My spouse must not lie to me." Lucy and Mark would have had a better morning if Mark had been more honest. It's possible that Mark did not want to be home with Lucy but didn't know how to be honest about his feelings. Mark might have been angry with her neediness and lack of respect for his work ethic. Lucy did not feel the need to listen to his side of the story, as she was convinced that Mark was wrong for breaking her rules. Her fury at his actions made meaningful discussion difficult.

We would all like our significant others to be more honest with us. Our marriages would be the better for it, and we could be more trusting of our partners and feel safer with them. The reality is that we cannot make our partners be more truthful with us than they choose to be. We cannot force our spouses to do anything they do not want to do. There is not much that Lucy can do if Mark wants to go to work badly enough that he is willing to lie about it.

Both Lucy and Bernice made themselves very unhappy because they could not accept some basic truths about their lives. Each woman kept on trying to enforce her unenforceable rules, despite the fact that her husband was unlikely to obey them. Each was certain that her rules were right and that her husband was wrong for disobeying them. They did not realize that you can't win when you are trying to enforce an unenforceable rule. Lucy and

Bernice got angry, but neither woman had the power to make her husband do what she wanted. This stress and frustration led to exaggerated feelings of anger and helplessness. Such feelings reduce the problem-solving capabilities because of neurochemical changes and impaired blood flow in the brain.

One of the major problems with unenforceable rules is that they are neither right nor reasonable. If they were reasonable, then people would follow them. Gordon's unenforceable rule was that Betty shouldn't nag him about sex. Betty's rule was that Gordon should have sex with her when she wanted him to. If these rules had been reasonable, Gordon would have had sex with Betty on demand because it would have been the right thing to do. Betty wouldn't have been a nag if her husband's rule against it had been legitimate. Why would Don drink if it was expressly against the rules? Clearly we and our spouses see and follow different rules. As an alcoholic, Don did exactly what alcoholics do: he drank whether or not he got his wife's permission.

Living with an alcoholic spouse is a troubling experience. Simply making better rules will not solve the problem. It may get so bad that you have to figure out what to do to protect yourself and your children. You need your wits about you to do this. When your mind is filled with helpless anger because your rules are not being followed, you have less energy available to think through your options. It is difficult enough to leave a spouse or obtain a restraining order. When we insist that our spouses do things they are not able to do—drink responsibly in this case—we only make the situation more challenging.

We create unenforceable rules in all aspects of our relationship, and they are at the root of most really bad marital trouble. Men and women often have different rules governing the same situation, and that can lead to all manner of problems. A wife might think, "I've had a hard day at work, and I need my husband to be understanding tonight and not pester me to have sex." But her husband approaches this situation with a different rule. He thinks, "I have had a hard day at work, and I need a loving and sexually available wife." Both partners are approaching this situation with an unenforceable rule.

Jane secretly considered her husband George an inconsiderate oaf. She inevitably got angry at him when he broke her rule and demanded sex too often. George saw things differently. He thought that Jane was being unkind when she turned down his sexual advances. As a result, Jane was often angry with George, while George felt shunned by Jane. When they stopped trying to enforce unenforceable rules and started forgiving each other, their marriage finally improved.

Insisting that your wife love you since you love her is an unenforceable rule. Why should she love you just because you love her? Demanding that your husband keep the house neat is an unenforceable rule. You can't expect him to want to keep the house neat just because you want it that way. And yes, your relationship would be easier if your husband was reliable, but why does he have to make life easier for you? Why does your wife have to offer you affection just because you want it? You can *want* good weather on your vacation, but *insisting* that it be so is an unenforceable rule. You can't influence the weather patterns simply by wanting a sunny day.

Each of these examples embodies a statement about what one spouse hopes will happen, and each consists of a good and positive wish: the world would be a better place if everyone was loved and treated fairly and the weather was always sunny. The problem comes when we forget that what we hope for is not the same as what we need or have the power to compel. Unenforceable rules warp our judgment. We try so hard to get our rules obeyed that we do not see the damage that ensues from that effort. We blame our lovers for breaking our rules, and we withhold our love when they do so. Our pain and frustration cause us to do things that harm our relationship rather than help it.

When we are upset, we rarely stop to examine whether our rules are enforceable. When we make an unenforceable rule in order to try to get what we want, our emotional frustration creates a secondary problem. Betty confused being with Gordon for ten years with a guarantee that he had to do what she wanted. She didn't realize that she had created an unenforceable rule and was acting as if wanting sex was the same as being owed sex on demand.

When we are upset, our thinking becomes cloudy. We become distracted and frazzled and don't realize that we are thinking unclearly. When we are thinking clearly, we remember to ask, "Is there a good probability that I will get what I want?" When clear-thinking individuals realize that they are unlikely to get what they want, they relax, work hard to discover alternatives, and hope for the best. Individuals who are not thinking clearly get mad, hurt, and frustrated; they become filled with a sense of blame, which leads to bitterness and hopelessness if not checked.

When our thinking becomes unclear, it is usually because we are trying to enforce an unenforceable rule. The problem we face is that there is almost no chance of getting an unenforceable rule to work. For example, Alex may demand with all of his might that his wife acknowledge his needs. However, if his wife chooses to ignore his needs, there is nothing Alex can do to change her. Rita may insist that her husband stop demanding sex every evening. However, if her husband chooses to keep demanding sex every night, there is nothing Rita can do to change him. Elaine can demand that her husband stop spoiling the kids. However, if her husband decides to keep on spoiling the kids, there is little Elaine can do to change him.

What you need to do in these kinds of situations is to construct rules that will lead to more peace and greater control over your emotions. The first step in unraveling your unenforceable rules is to recognize them. When you finally realize that you are making unenforceable rules, you are taking the first step toward helping yourself. Simply by doing this, you have taken back some of the power you gave your spouse to hurt you. This is true whether your spouse failed, or was selfish, or stood firm defending his or her quirky behavior, or loved you wrong, or forgot your birthday.

When you challenge your unenforceable rules, you take the next step in learning to forgive. The good news is that challenging unenforceable rules is a simple process. Unenforceable rules make their presence known. You do not have to look far to find them. *Every* time you are more than mildly upset with the actions of your lover, it is because you are trying to enforce an unenforceable rule. *Every* time you are more than mildly upset with your life, it is because you are trying to enforce an unenforceable rule. *Every* time you are more than mildly upset with yourself, you are trying to enforce an unenforceable rule.

People stay angry or hurt only when an unenforceable rule has been broken. If you feel angry, bitter, depressed, alienated, enraged, or hopeless, then you are dealing with this situation. You will still experience sadness and frustration even if you get rid of the unenforceable rules in your relationship, but having these feelings isn't wrong. What you need to realize is that underneath your most painful feelings are rules you are helplessly trying to enforce. Once you start to challenge your rules when you first feel upset, then your bad feelings won't last and will not be as severe.

The first step to change your unenforceable rules is to become upset when they are broken. Doing this is as easy as getting mad when your lover puts the dishes away in the wrong place again. Monique got mad because her partner Henry broke the rule about putting the plates back where she wanted them to go. Did Monique have the power to stop Henry from doing that? No. Was her rule enforceable? No. The result: anger and frustration. The only thing Monique could do was tell her friends and family about Henry's annoying habits. However, this only served to hurt her emotional health and mental well-being and destroy her peace of mind.

Taking the first step toward challenging your unenforceable rules is as simple as remembering how little you have felt loved lately. When Dave came to see me, he was dealing with problems with his wife. She was angry and always demanding that he pay more attention to their kids. Dave worked hard, had a difficult commute, and was tired when he got home. He was frustrated that his wife seemed to have so little patience with his daily struggle to provide for his family. When he thought about her yelling at him, he felt tense and angry. Dave's rule was that a good wife must be understanding and sensitive to her husband's needs. This was a legitimate desire—but a lousy rule. Dave had no power to force his wife to comply with his vision of a good spouse.

I led Dave through the first two steps of challenging his unenforceable rule. The first step was to acknowledge that he was upset and that what was upsetting him was occurring right now. By doing this, he was acknowledging that the pain was current; therefore, he was trying to enforce the unenforceable rules right now. The second step was to realize that his unhappiness was a result of both the situation and his frustration at being unable to enforce an unenforceable rule. I told Dave that his unenforceable rule was a bigger problem to him than his wife. Trying to force your spouse to be a different person would upset and anger anyone. Insisting that your spouse develop sensitivity and patience he or she may not possess only leads to frustration. I pointed out to Dave that his wife's behavior was common. Many people have spouses who pick fights, so rules like his are often broken.

I explained to Dave that his suffering was the result of turning his desire for a specific kind of sensitive wife into a rule that his wife had to follow. Wanting a kind wife was a legitimate wish. Insisting on it in a specific form was a recipe for disaster.

Step three for Dave was to be willing to challenge the unenforceable rules that were causing him so much pain. Instead of focusing on his wife's behavior, Dave needed to focus on changing the way he thought about it. Once Dave realized how much pain his unenforceable rules were causing, he was willing to try anything to fix things.

Uncovering the unenforceable rule is the fourth step in the process, and it is much easier than you may think. The unenforceable rule is simply the desire or hope you have for something good that you have turned into an expectation or demand. The desire could be for love, safety, sex, shared child raising, support, friendship, loyalty, money, back scratching, or good conversation. All Dave really wanted was an indulgent and sensitive partner, but he turned that wish into a demand. Rita desired a less lustful husband, but she turned that wish into a demand for less sex. None of us have the ability to force our lovers to comply with our demands, and therefore they often break our rules. It can be difficult to accept the fact that your lover does not have to make your life easier or better or lessen your suffering when you want him or her to. You will only suffer more, however, when you try harder to enforce your unenforceable rules rather than challenge them.

Ask yourself who or what in your relationship must change for you to be happy, and you will discover your unenforceable rules. Ask yourself these questions:

- Am I demanding that my partner treat me better than he/
  she does?

- Am I demanding that my past with my partner be better
  than it was?

- Am I demanding that my life with my partner be easier
  than it is?

- Am I demanding that our relationship be fairer than I feel
  it is?

When you find yourself thinking in any of these ways, you
have pinpointed an unenforceable rule.

Once you've identified your unenforceable rule, you need to
figure out how to hold on to the enforceable desire and get rid of
the unenforceable demand. Hoping that things will go the way
you want and working hard to get your wishes gratified is a
good approach to your relationship. At the same time, remind
yourself that you cannot control your lover's behavior, and it is
foolish to demand things that your lover isn't willing to give. Try
substituting the words "hope" or "wish" for "must" or "have to"
in your unenforceable expectation or demand. This will help you
avoid driving yourself crazy and retain the energy to maximize
the relationship you have.

I suggested that Betty rephrase her rule and say that she *hoped*
for a lover who was always sexually available, rather than that
her lover *had* to always be sexually available. She could still express her wishes, but now she could realize that happiness re-
sided in accepting Gordon for who he was. This acceptance,
coupled with nonangry and nondefensive efforts to talk about sex
with Gordon, would help her marriage. Betty needed to remember that she loved her husband, not her demands. I suggest the

same to you all. A week later, Betty told me that she felt better but was struggling to get used to a different way of thinking. I assured her that in time she would get used to this way of thinking that leads to forgiveness and a much-improved relationship.

Challenging your unenforceable rules lets you take responsibility for your feelings and helps you take your partner's quirks less personally. You become aware that much of what you took personally about your partner's behavior was only rules you could not enforce. You remember that you love your partner, not the things you are demanding from him or her. Once you do this, you can see that your thinking played a significant role in the anger and hurt that you felt. As you challenge your rules, you will see that clearer thinking leads to more peaceful coexistence in your marriage and day-to-day life.

Six Steps to Challenge Your Unenforceable Rules

1. Recognize that you feel hurt, angry, alienated, depressed, or hopeless. Acknowledge that your feelings may be from memories of the past, but that you are experiencing them in the present.

2. Remind yourself that you feel bad because you are currently trying to enforce an unenforceable rule.

3. Assert your willingness to challenge your unenforceable rule right now.

4. Find your unenforceable rule by asking yourself, "What aspects of my relationship am I insisting must change from how they actually are?"

5. Change the way you think about these issues from demanding that you get what you want to hoping that you get what you want.

6. Notice that when you wish or hope that things will be a certain way, you think more clearly and are more peaceful than when you demand that they be a certain way.

I want to end this chapter with a short list of some of the most common unenforceable rules. I'll also give you some simple strategies to challenge the rules, and I'll show you how couples can learn healthier ways of thinking. This is not an exhaustive list of unenforceable rules, nor are these the only ways to challenge unenforceable rules. This list is only a guide to show you some common rules and some more realistic ways of looking at life.

1. *My partner has to be faithful....* Alan found it was more realistic to say he hoped his wife would be faithful. He had learned the hard way that she had to choose to be faithful and he could not force her to do so. In a subsequent relationship, Alan learned how precious that choice of faithfulness is, and he committed himself to appreciate the gift. Alan had the best chance, but no guarantee, of experiencing his wife's faithfulness by treating her with kindness and respect. He learned that there is a risk in offering love and trust. He found that there are no guarantees, but that the rewards are great.

2. *My lover must not lie to me....* Beatrice found it more realistic to say that she hoped Don would be truthful. However, she saw numerous examples of his deceit and learned to ask

herself why her husband should be immune from a common human problem. She learned that husbands and wives and marriage are complex and that people do all sorts of selfish and destructive things when they are under stress. As long as Beatrice demanded otherwise, she was foolhardy and suffered accordingly.

3. *Relationships should be fair....* Mary learned the hard way that it was more realistic to hope that relationships are fair. Shortly after she married Sam, he fell sick and was out of work for two and a half years. Mary constantly complained that "life is not fair." She would have been a happy camper if she had gotten the final say about who gets sick and who does not. Unfortunately, she was not part of that decision-making team. Just as in a twelve-step program, she had to "learn to deal with life on life's terms."

4. *People have to treat me with kindness or care in the way I want....* Both Nathan and Janet demanded that their spouses treat them with more kindness. Both forgot that they could not force this behavior in another person. Each of them was married to a partner who often spoke bluntly and had a gruff exterior. However, their spouses were also loyal and hardworking partners and parents. Both Nathan and Janet had to learn that demanding specific acts and tokens of kindness from a spouse who cannot give them that way is foolhardy. They needed to focus more on their lovers' good qualities than their bad ones.

5. *My marriage should be easy....* It is natural and great to hope for good times and pleasant experiences, but dangerous to expect them. Jerry and his wife lived in a very expensive neighborhood, and he had to work two jobs to make ends meet. His wife worked too, so they had very little time

together, and they missed each other. Jerry felt very sorry
for himself until he looked around and saw that every
marriage had its challenges. So he changed his thinking to
"I would love an easy life, but until I get one, I will
appreciate the one I have."

6. *My past with my lover should have been different.* ... This is the
most common unenforceable rule I see, and the simplest to
challenge. Remember, the past is done, and all you have is
your current relationship. Jacob still felt that his wife
should not have had an affair. Sally still felt that Joe had
been too harsh with her parents. Jacob was able to
challenge his unenforceable rule and say, "I would have
liked my wife to have been faithful, but if I want the
marriage, I must deal with my loss." Sally was able to say,
"I wish Joe had been kinder to my parents, but the past is
done and we will start anew."

———◆———

SEVEN

Step 3:
Let Your Partner Know
How Blessed You Are

In chapters 5 and 6, I advised you to make peace with the reality that we choose our lovers with free will and must accept that, being human beings, they are bound to disappoint us occasionally and to make decisions that we don't like and can't control. Some of their decisions may be hurtful, and some may just be different from what we had hoped. If you have found someone you think is a "keeper," then you need to forgive and to love this person. This chapter and the next explore the flip side of your partner's freedom to choose how to act. Here I focus on your ability to see that the good your lover offers is freely given and often remarkably loving and that love itself is marvelous. Your lover's freedom to choose allows you to exult and find meaning and beauty in your lover's kindness, love, loyalty, and generosity.

The freedom to choose gives both partners space for the effort, discipline, love, and hard work that go into creating a loving relationship. This chapter is about recognizing that both you and your partner regularly exercise the freedom to do good, to love, and to be kind. Bob had the freedom to choose to listen to his wife as she struggled with her mother's slowly worsening dementia. Sally had the freedom to focus on what her partner did wrong or on what she did right. It is how both partners in a relationship use their freedom of choice that ultimately determines the quality of the love between them.

Sadly, we are more likely to notice our partners' choices when we are angry at them rather than when we are pleased. And in fact our lovers may continue to taunt us even though they know it drives us crazy. They can choose to stop or not stop. Mike could take his car out on a snowy night and crash it, even when his wife had told him not to. Dave's wife might neglect the housework even after he had told her how much it bothered him. Joan could continue to be late even when her partner Jordan begged her to be on time. We need to see our lovers' selfishness or laziness or inability to complete tasks they have begun. It is only by seeing what our lovers' limits are that we can help them or share our concerns. The thing that cripples relationships is focusing more on their flaws than on their loving or their goodness. This misplaced attention makes no sense and underlies many of our difficulties with forgiveness.

Every spouse has enormous good to offer to the other one; when we don't pay attention to those gifts, we can kill the marriage. We ignore the endless piles of laundry she cleans and folds, the jobs he goes to year after year, the ongoing effort she makes to tolerate our flaws. Our anger blinds us to the ways in which our partner overcame his childhood difficulties to be a productive person, her simple dignity in how she acts under stress, or what a loving father he is. We miss both the small indications of love we regularly receive and the larger moments that sustain our lives. The list of our lover's good qualities is endless and limited only by our effort and imagination. We take our lovers and relationships for granted and do not notice our blessings until something goes wrong.

In forgiveness classes I compare the way we treat our partners with the way we treat our cars. When our cars are dirty or broken, they catch our attention. We grumble a little, then bring the car into the shop to be repaired or have someone go out and clean it. When the car starts and gets us where we are going, we don't think about it. A smoothly running car is just doing what we expect of it. We are rarely thankful when the car starts on a cold or rainy night, but we are very attentive when our car is broken. Some marriages are like the perfect second car that Rodney Dangerfield jokes about—a tow truck. Their relationship is so neglected that it is constantly in danger of getting towed to the shop. Many of us, however, expect our lovers to love us day after day, and it doesn't really occur to us to be thankful when they do so.

We also think about our cars when we have to buy gas: instead of appreciating how little effort it takes to keep the car going, we complain about the price of filling it up. In addition, we pay more attention to our car when we see that someone else has a better one. Speeding down the freeway, we catch a glimpse of a fancier or newer car and all of a sudden we have a problem with our own vehicle. Our car may have given us years of service, but when we see a better car we want that one instead. I am afraid that many people have a similar relationship with their partner. They expect their partner to provide love and care, and it is only when things go wrong that they notice the state of their relationship. Instead of thanking their partner for the years of care, they look outside the relationship to find a better model. Nothing could be more deadly to a relationship.

Love suffers when we focus on our partners' difficult traits and problematic behaviors to the exclusion of their beauty and goodness. We accentuate our painful experiences when we focus our attention on difficult traits. By focusing on what is wrong, we immediately put stress into our bodies and minds. By taking our partners' good qualities for granted and focusing on their errors and flaws, we create more stress in our lives and relationship. That stress contributes to disordered thinking and disturbed relationships. As a result, we miss the enormous number of good and loving choices our partners make every day. What brings love to our relationship and sows the seeds for forgiveness is simple: appreciating absolutely everything we can about the person we are with each and every day. There is nothing simpler to do, and no more powerful gift you can offer to your partner.

Once you focus on the idea of your lover having free will, you can see how many choices, positive or negative, your lover makes. He or she is an independent person and can choose many paths of action, some of which you will not like. Your lover has the freedom to make annoying and painful choices, at the cost of your relationship. The blessing of this situation is seeing the enormous number of loving choices your lover makes daily. Our failure to notice the endless stream of generous actions is the deepest flaw we bring to our marriages. When our lovers offer us goodness or kindness, it is because they choose to do it. They don't have to be good or kind, and their gift is the fact that they made those choices when they did not have to. Human nature is often selfish and insensitive, but we are all capable of also being remarkably generous and kind. In most marriages the spouses offer each other more good than bad, but too often we take the good for granted.

The hard truth is that at this very moment your lover could decide that you are not worth any further effort. You have no power over the decisions your partner makes, and demanding something that he or she does not wish to give is an unenforceable rule. Our vulnerability to our lovers' whims makes forgiving them hard, and that is what makes relationships so difficult. Once we have been hurt, we fear that they could hurt us again. We worry that they might not change for the better and could even change for the worse.

The overlooked upside is that we are vulnerable to their goodness as well. And once we start to look, we realize all the good our lovers do. At the end of the day, the only thing we have power over is how much we ourselves do to help the marriage; we cannot control our lovers' actions. The best thing we can do is to use our power to appreciate our lovers so that we have many reasons to forgive them their trespasses and flaws. You can dramatically improve your chances for success in your relationship if you simply give thanks for being loved numerous times each day. Try to notice the little things your lover does every day to make the relationship work. Be thankful for every day he or she tolerates you with all your quirks and wounds. You want to see your partner's goodness and forgiveness and honor the effort he or she makes to care for you. Try to notice your lover's strengths and good points and kind actions as often as possible. Tell your lover how lucky you are that he or she chose you for a partner and continues to choose you every single day.

Your marriage will also be helped if you appreciate the gifts of your life together. Be proud of your home and revel in the bounty of food and clothing and shelter you share. Honor the achievements of your children and praise your partner for his input and effort. It is important to realize the preciousness of life and never take it for granted. Waking up next to a person who loves you is a blessing, so don't just rush by it. Take a moment to silently give thanks. Let your partner know that you appreciate her sexual desire for you. Be humble enough to realize that the fact that your partner picked you out of the six billion people on earth is a blessing. That blessing of love is the most remarkable experience of your life.

Our partner's choice to care for us is the most precious gift we will ever receive, the richest treasure we can have, and the most exquisite indication of human goodness. It is this beautiful because it can only be offered freely and cannot be coerced. The gift of love is a mystery that we will never fully understand. Everything our partner offers us is generously offered and needs to be received as such. All of our life has been a preparation to be a safe place for someone to love. We need to be the kind of person who can see the gift in love and honor our lover with kindness and devotion. One of the worst flaws of human nature is our inability to pay sufficient attention to our lovers' gift of themselves to us. We do this in part because we are trying to force them to do things that are not under our control.

Real love can emerge only when there is choice. If Sam is obliged to treat Carly exactly as she demands to be treated, then what is there for Sam to do but follow instructions? If Carly gets to make all the decisions, then Sam is not really a full partner. It is only real choice that allows romantic love to flourish. Jack can tell Jill he will love her for the rest of his life, but he still has to wake up every day and do so. If she hovers over him and rates his love for her by the hour, it will quickly be extinguished. Jack will get tired of the judgments and the pressure to perform. We cannot be forced to love. As much as choice is a responsibility, it also provides the freedom to love and care and forgive. The risks we take when we choose to love one particular person and the resulting uncertainty are the ground upon which true love emerges.

How remarkable is it that your lover continues to spend time with you, listen to you, and try to make your relationship work of his or her own free will? How wonderful is it that your lover continues to have sex with you and to parent your children? Your lover's devotion and willingness to plug away day after day when there are sleeker and newer models to meet is a blessing. We need to let our lovers know how amazing they are and how grateful we are. We need to make offering gratitude a priority in our lives and our marriages. Try giving your partner simple tokens of love, schedule appreciation in your datebook or PDA, and send text messages showing that you notice and appreciate your lover's affection. This should be a goal every day that you are with your beloved.

Forgiveness rests on our ability to see enough of the good in our lovers to keep their bad qualities in perspective. Our lovers' faults—like driving recklessly or drinking or not paying child support—are often forced upon our attention, but we have to choose to notice the good things about them; when they are humbly going to work or making meals or doing the grocery shopping, they are doing nothing that forces us to pay attention. Reacting to danger or loss is hardwired into our nervous system, but appreciating our partner takes a conscious effort. We need to make that effort to honor our partner over and over.

When you feel grateful for your lover, you are able to feel forgiving toward him or her. Forgiveness is a positive emotion that can actually restore some of the damage done to your body by anger and stress. When you are focused on your problems and grievances, your body is under stress. Your stress chemicals are active, and you feel tired and beaten down. You blame the offender for your distress and feel disempowered. Feeling grateful and forgiving can wash away the stress and relax your body and mind.

Stress causes your body to tighten up and your brain to constrict; positive emotions like forgiveness and gratitude have the opposite effect. The blood that drains away from the thinking part of your brain when you are stressed returns when you feel grateful or forgiving. When blood flows unimpeded in the front part of the brain, your thinking is at its best. You can then solve the problems you face with less anger and frustration. Positive emotion increases your ability to think creatively and with flexibility. Feelings of gratitude and forgiveness also help your heart rate slow down, lower your blood pressure, increase the health of your immune system, and balance your nervous system. Your entire mind-body system benefits when you feel positive emotion.

We often start to hold a grudge because we are focusing more on the pain our partners have caused and less on their gifts and good qualities. Sometimes our complaints are caused by nothing more than forgetting the love we have been given. We continue to hold our grudges when we do not keep our lovers' goodness front and center. When we forgive our partners, we see more than just the harm they may have done. Not that they are blameless or perfect. But when we forgive them, we can see them fully enough to lose the need to punish them for their failures. When we forgive them, we appreciate their goodness so much that we can have the necessary yet difficult conversations without bitterness.

Research has shown that two partners remember the negatives in their relationship more than the positives and that most couples need to have around five positive experiences for each negative one in order for the relationship to work. Appreciating our partners' good qualities is a great way to rebalance a marriage that has too much anger and stress, and it's something we can easily do many times a day to balance out negativity. We offer our partners a great gift by acknowledging the good they do and all they bring to our lives.

We become more forgiving when we look deeply into the mystery of love and are humbled as a result. Once we think about it, we realize that we have done nothing that is enough to explain the gift of true love. Lovers who really listen, are patient and kind, or show us that they adore us every day are not doing so because they have to. They are offering us these gifts because they love us, not because we have done something to earn them. Love is more than the sum of our good qualities, and it can't be explained by looking at a balance sheet. Our good deeds and kind words go a long way toward making our partners act lovingly toward us. However, our deeds and speech are not sufficient by themselves. We need to remain open to the mystery and gift of love.

Your ability to forgive grows stronger when you accept the gifts of love your partner offers. At the very least this means accepting that your relationship will not last forever. This also means that you should glorify any and all experiences you have of love. One way to do this is to understand that love is a precious gift and to be grateful for the fact that you were given it, even if it did not last. One of the tragedies I see in my work is people discounting past love because it did not last. They are unable to take joy in the love they shared because that love ended. I have had numerous people tell me that their marriage of twenty years was a sham because after fifteen years their partner had an affair. Their pain was understandable, but it minimized the fact that the love in their lives was majestic and a blessing no matter how long it lasted.

Understanding that everybody has good and bad habits and different tendencies and skills will help you to become more forgiving. Your wife may be a wonderful parent and a lousy cook. Your husband may be terrific at tasks that require physical exertion, like taking care of the car, but useless at cleaning up the kitchen. Your lover may be great at discussing ideas and lousy at discussing feelings. If you pay more attention to your partner's weaknesses than to his or her strengths, you deny yourself joy and make it much harder to forgive your partner's flaws. Instead, you should be generous with your praise and notice your partner's bad qualities without getting lost in them. You want to appreciate your partner's good points and deal as successfully as possible with the bad points. Flipping your attention this way will help you develop a forgiving attitude toward your lover.

Being forgiving does not require you to be oblivious to your partner's flaws. But it will help you refrain from obsessing over your partner's problems and enable you to focus on the big picture instead, in the realization that your partner has been loyal to you for a significant period of time. Your lover craves your acknowledgment and wants desperately to be noticed for the good he or she does. You can put the things that annoy you about your lover into perspective if you think about your lover's kind nature, or the wonderful way your lover treats your parents. It is easier to address your lover's flaws with kindness if you genuinely appreciate his or her good qualities.

You need to learn to appreciate your partner in three different ways in order to truly foster forgiveness between the two of you. The first way is to recognize the specific good your lover does for you. Look for all the ways, both big and small, in which your lover serves you and makes your life better. Perhaps she happily worked overtime to pay for a vacation, or maybe he made love even when he was tired. Maybe your lover always lets you pick the movie, or makes you dinner when you are sick. Try to appreciate the household work your lover gets done: doing the laundry three times a week, mowing the lawn, making sure the bills are paid. Maybe your lover takes responsibility for doing the grocery shopping, making play dates for the kids, or getting all the dishes put away. It's also very important to acknowledge and appreciate the sex, communication, and physical affection you share with your lover.

You might want to consider these questions when looking for things to appreciate in your lover:

1. How does my partner show me that he/she is my friend?

2. How does my partner show me that he/she is my lover?

3. How does my partner show me that I'm special?

4. How does my partner show me that he/she appreciates me?

5. How does my partner show me that he/she loves me?

When people are reminded to appreciate their partners, their grievances often melt away. I asked Dave to spend three minutes telling me all the reasons he was lucky to live with Mary. As he struggled, I asked him leading questions about who listens to him when he needs to talk, who sleeps with him, and who does most of the laundry, cooking, and cleaning. Then I asked him to make a second list of Mary's attributes, but not to repeat anything from his first list. By this time, Dave's face had grown more relaxed and open. Mary was also in the room, and as she observed Dave, her face softened too. Soon Dave was able to talk to Mary with an understanding of how much she meant to him. After Dave was done talking, Mary turned to him and told him she was also sorry for taking him and their relationship for granted.

The second way to appreciate our lovers is to look for the good they do in the world by acknowledging the help they give to other people, the care they offer our children, or the good they do at work or volunteering. By appreciating the contribution our lovers make, we acknowledge that their lives have meaning and are important. Try to look for all the different successes your lover has achieved at work and at home. I asked Debbie to pretend that her husband Danny had been nominated for a humanitarian award and to make a list of all the good he did in his life. Debbie needed to highlight all the people he helped in his job and the many ways in which he served his parents, his children, and his community. I wanted her to acknowledge the hero she had married.

It is important to be your lover's biggest fan and most enduring cheerleader. Look carefully so that you see how much your lover accomplishes in a day. It is easy to find something to honor, as we all do so much that goes unnoticed every day. If you can't find something, either you are not good at looking or you may have made a poor choice of partner. Look at the movie *It's a Wonderful Life,* which tells the story of a hardworking and community-minded man who feels he has been a failure in life. The central theme of the movie is simple but profound: no one has failed who has helped others and loved his family. That should be a message we each give our partners on a regular basis.

The third way to appreciate our lovers is to look for and praise their good qualities by telling them how much we admire how they think, behave, and react. We need to appreciate the everyday good qualities that often go unnoticed, like honesty, thrift, gentleness, courage, and kindness. It is so easy to take your lover for granted and to start missing the person you married.

One exercise I often do with clients goes like this. First I have the client write down five positive words that best describe his or her partner. Then I ask the client to give me specific examples of these attributes.

One of Jerry's five words about his wife Kim was "kind," so I then asked him for a specific example of her kindness. When he told me something she did for him, I asked him to follow up with a story about something she did for someone else. The more Jerry could see Kim's good qualities and praise them, the less likely he was to exaggerate the struggle of being married. Every time I work with a couple I focus on the need to notice the ways in which each partner is a good human being. Another client, Lisa, took her husband's self-discipline for granted, while Samantha failed to see her husband's consistent loyalty to her. I then asked each woman to tell me stories of times when her partner had used his good qualities to be kind or helpful toward her. After this exercise, we talked about their resentments again, and this time there was a little less bite and more forgiveness in the women's answers.

Appreciating our lovers and telling them how wonderful they can be are great ways to take responsibility for the health of our marriages. It is important to continue to make an effort to appreciate the good in your partner and relationship, even if you are in pain at the time. When you do this, the balanced perspective puts you in a better position to make decisions. The common tendency is to feel that your experience of hurt is more real than your ability to love. It is important to challenge this belief and also to challenge the very human tendency to say that the painful experiences your spouse caused go deeper than the love you feel for them. The pain you feel will diminish in importance when you bring more positive experiences into your relationship.

I created a simple guided visualization/meditation to help you keep connected to the good in your lover and relationship. This practice reminds you of your partner's good points and reduces stress. It is also a gentle way to stay connected with your lover when you are not together or when you feel a bit estranged. This is a guided visualization that you can do anytime you want to feel close to your lover or want to reduce some stress you feel in your relationship.

Lovers' Appreciation

1. At least two or three times every day, slow down and put your attention on the rise and fall of your belly as you breathe. Specifically, as you inhale, allow the air to gently expand your belly until it is full.

2. Keeping your neck, shoulders, and belly soft and relaxed, exhale and watch your belly fall as the air is pushed out.

3. Continue breathing this way for two or three more slow deep breaths.

4. Then, for each of the next three to five inhalations, picture in your mind's eye your lover at his/her best, or picture some special way your lover cares for you.

5. As you picture your lover, try to feel the love you have for him/her and say the words "thank you" silently to yourself. You may have a stronger response if you imagine your experience of gratitude as centered in your heart.

6. After these five "appreciation breaths," return to the breathing from steps one and two for one more breath and then gently resume your regular activity.

Another practice I teach to strengthen and broaden my clients' appreciation of their lovers uses the metaphor of a TV remote control. Imagine that what you see in your mind is being viewed on a TV screen—what you see and hear is part of a TV program. On your TV screen at home you can choose the programs you want to see, and you can change channels with your remote control: you can flip between a horror movie on channel 4 and a nature program on channel 14, and if you feel like watching sports, you can select channel 51. You have control of the remote, so you can determine what appears on your TV.

Imagine now that you have a remote control that changes the channel you are viewing in your mind. The pictures in your mind can be changed in the same way you change the channel of your TV. By controlling the remote, you can decide what kinds of experiences you have. Looking at it this way, you can see that if you are having endless grievances with your partner, it is because your remote control is stuck on the grievance channel. Dorothy was stuck watching endless reruns of the *My Husband Should Have Loved Me More* show. All that ever seemed to be showing on Mike's TV were repeat episodes of *Women Can't Be Trusted*. Those of us who have persistent, long-term problems with our partner probably feel that the only button that works on our remote control is the one that tunes us into the grievance channel.

I challenge the people I work with to reprogram their remote controls so as to regularly tune in to the channels that open their hearts and help them connect with their lovers. By doing this, they can appreciate both their lovers and all the other amazing things they are grateful for in their lives. The goodness, love, beauty, courage, and kindness channels are always available for viewing.

Sarah's husband Tom may have been a careless, lazy, and limited parent, but that didn't mean she had to keep her remote control stuck on the grievance channel of bad parenting.

Sarah knew that there was real love shared between them, they had great sex, and Tom was a friendly and warm man. She also realized that she made enough money for them to live comfortably. She knew that if she pushed Tom enough, he would do more—she just resented that she had to make so much effort to get him to help out. In our meetings, I didn't want to talk about what Sarah could do about Tom; I just wanted to help her get her remote unstuck. We also worked together to help Sarah remember goodness in its many forms. With some practice, Sarah realized that she had more control over how she felt than she realized. Equally importantly, she started to learn how to control the amount of stress her body held. Finally, she saw that her hostility toward Tom was not that endearing.

Because I work in California, I often ask people to pay attention to natural beauty instead of watching reruns of their old grudges. I ask people to dust off what I call the "Big Sur" channel. Big Sur is an area on the California coast where nature is stupendous and the views are gorgeous. Like Yosemite National Park or the Grand Canyon, Big Sur is a place of such magnificent beauty that it is hard to be there and stay in a bad mood. I ask those in my classes to occasionally tune in to the Big Sur channel as a reminder that the beauty of nature is always nearby and their lives are not over. Looking at nature in this way also helps us realize that the world is bigger than our problems. The joy and majesty of a place like Big Sur is as real as any hurt or disappointment. And it is just a button away on the remote.

I have spent much of this chapter talking about getting better at tuning in your love channel. Beyond that, the world is full of things to appreciate and find beautiful once you teach yourself to look. The forgiveness and gratitude channels remind us that even though we have been hurt, we do not have to dwell on the hurt. The one thing no one can take from us is what we pay attention to and focus on. We may have a habit of watching the grievance channel or the bitterness channel, but we still control the remote. The good news is that, with practice, any habit can be broken or changed. The world is full of heroes who have overcome difficulty by tuning in to channels of courage or bravery. Each of us can become a hero in our own life, to the benefit of our friends and family.

Here are some suggestions to help you start tuning in to your gratitude channel. As you notice and affirm these blessings in your life, you will need six to ten seconds for the effect to take place. Our bodies are wired to respond to danger faster than we can think about actually doing anything. The instant we see or think of danger, the stress response kicks in and we are alert. The alert state lasts until things are good and our body can relax and an "all-clear" is sounded. To relax, our bodies need six to eight seconds of positive thinking or attention. That means that if you are going to appreciate your husband when you are mad at him, you have to hold his love for you in your mind for up to ten seconds before the thought relaxes you.

- Walk into your nearest supermarket or health food store and give thanks for the abundance of food available.

- When you go into any large shopping area or store, marvel at the choices available and how little you have to do to purchase things.

- Pass by a nursing home or hospital and give thanks for your good health.

- When driving, mentally thank each driver who follows the rules of the road.

- If you have a good friend, thank that person for caring for you.

- Remind yourself of any kindnesses done by your parents.

- Notice a salesperson or store clerk and thank that person for waiting on you.

- In your home, give thanks for all of the labor that went into making your furniture, appliances, and food.

- When you wake up each morning, give thanks for your breath and the gift of your life.

- Notice the gifts of nature on a regular basis.

To create a new habit you need to practice it. The more you repeat this new habit, the easier it becomes, and the more it feels part of your true nature. If you practice being grateful throughout the day it will become easier and easier to actually *be* grateful. The more you complain about your husband the easier it becomes to complain. Similarly, the more you praise your husband the easier it becomes to think of him as deserving praise. To create a new habit you also need to use what is called a "transfer of learning": using a skill you learned to do one task to do a second, similar task. For instance, the more goodness you can find in life, the easier it is to find goodness in your lover. The more goodness you find in your lover, the easier it is to find it in your life.

Although I put a strong emphasis on gratitude and positive experiences, I am not suggesting that they alone will solve all your problems or make your marriage blissful. You may still have to confront your lover for misbehavior or lack of productive activity, and you may still have to make some hard choices about your relationship. What a positive outlook does do is allow you to put your difficulties into perspective. This in turn gives you access to feelings of forgiveness. Positive emotions clear your mind and heart so that you have the best chance of making good decisions and maintaining a good relationship. Practicing gratitude also makes it less likely that you will say things in anger that you later regret, or forget why you chose to love your spouse in the first place.

There are going to be times when you are so frustrated with your lover that there is no way you are going to access his or her good points in a meditation. The following breathing visualization has been altered to allow you to concentrate on something other than your loved one. Even though you are not focusing on your partner in this exercise, any appreciation makes overall forgiveness easier. Once again, use the six to nine breaths to ensure a positive effect in your nervous system.

Breathing in Appreciation

1. *At least two or three times every day, slow down and put your attention on your stomach. As you inhale, allow the air to gently expand your belly until it is full. As you do this, keep your shoulders and neck relaxed.*

2. *When you exhale and your belly goes down, make sure your belly stays soft and relaxed as you release the air.*

3. *Continue breathing this way for two or three slow deep breaths.*

4. *For each of the next three to five inhalations, picture some kind of goodness: a beautiful scene in nature, the gift of friendship, the simple joy of being alive.*

5. *As you picture your goodness, say the words "thank you" silently to yourself. You may have a stronger response if you imagine your experience of gratitude as centered in your heart.*

6. *After these five "appreciation breaths," return to the simple belly breathing from step one for one more breath and then gently resume your regular activity.*

I want to end this chapter with a story about Helen. During our work together, Helen learned how to use gratitude, and eventually gratitude was a central part of her forgiveness of her

old relationship and creation of a new one. Helen was an attractive woman in her late thirties who was going out with
Stan. Her last boyfriend had dumped her for her sister, and
she was still livid and filled with rage at both of them. During
our classes it became clear that Helen felt at her best when she
was plotting revenge on her sister or simply wailing about her
mistreatment in this painful situation. It was an ugly, compli-
cated situation.

Helen clearly had a chip on her shoulder about what had happened. I could see tears forming in her eyes, even though she
mostly just sat quietly and listened to the group. When she did
speak, she insisted that the hurt she had suffered was not repair-
able and there was no possibility she would ever forgive her boyfriend and sister for breaking her heart. She was incredibly angry
and let anyone within earshot know that her sister was a disrep-
utable louse and her ex should be castrated.

One day I asked Helen why she was upset when neither her
sister nor her ex was in the room. She looked at me like I was
crazy. I told her, "Helen, I don't see anyone or anything in this
room to be upset with. Nevertheless, I see you are unhappy.
Where does that come from?" I gently raised the idea that she
might have simply formed a habit of being upset and that she
had gotten used to feeling these negative emotions. Helen struggled
to understand that if she spent two hours a day lamenting her
loss, she would feel small and victimized. Adding in the fact that
she spent no time reflecting on things to be grateful for, her unhappiness was inevitable.

I told Helen that her pained response was a common reaction
to the kind of hurt she had suffered. She had created a habit of
keeping her sister and her ex and the betrayal and mistreatment
she had experienced on her mind. I then led the class through a
guided visualization on fully appreciating a person they knew

loved them. I asked them to explore the gift of love and to feel the positive experience in their hearts. This was an in-class demonstration of how to use their remote control to change their TVs to the gratitude channel. At the end of the visualization, I asked Helen how she felt. Helen admitted that she felt better, but that it had nothing to do with forgiveness. The next step in the exercise was to have the class write down three positive feelings that the presence of their lovers in their lives had given them and to give specific examples of each feeling. When Helen was done writing about Stan, I asked her how she felt. She again admitted that she felt good. Finally I asked her, "If you could bring up those peaceful feelings when you are upset at Stan, would that make a difference in your life?" After thinking about it, she finally said that doing this exercise probably would help her feel more peaceful and in less pain. It was great to see her make progress; I told her that she was right and that she was on to something important.

One way of looking at forgiveness is to see it as the conscious practice of extending and deepening moments of peace. For Helen, forgiveness meant learning to change her TV channel from the grievance show to something a little more positive. She finally realized that her current happy relationship was more important than the failed one in her past. She saw that it was healthier to focus on the people who loved her than on the ones who did not. The bottom line was that Helen was able to forgive her betrayal when she focused on positive experiences, such as moments of gratitude or love. She still had more work to do, but if she continued to practice and integrate those moments of peaceful feeling into her life, Helen was going to move a long way toward forgiveness.

It is important to create a positive present and to stop endlessly replaying the past.

Helen learned that how she felt was directly related to what was playing on her TV. She felt overwhelmed with pain when she focused all her attention on her disloyal sister and the loss of her love. This pain kept her stuck in the past, which prevented her new relationship from really taking off. When she started the class, Helen knew that she had a great new guy who might be a "keeper," but she was unable to commit to him. Once she was able to forgive her sister and her ex, she was able to look at her new relationship with an open, unafraid heart.

Helen learned this simple truth: her sister and her ex had no power over her when she felt good and peaceful. I asked her to understand that her goal was to extend the power of those peaceful moments. By working toward this goal, she would feel increasingly able to guide her moods and thoughts and develop a more forgiving nature. You can achieve the same goal as long as you appreciate the good in your life rather than regret or resent the bad. The power of appreciation will heal your life and empower your relationship.

◆

EIGHT

Step 4:
To Know Them Is to Love Them

For the first time in this book, we will now look directly at a quality of our partner's that we do not like. We will explore our lovers' flaws and failures and try to learn to see them through loving eyes. This step is different from the previous three, which simply ask you to acknowledge that you chose a particular flawed person and urge you to see your lover's good points. In this step, you will be asked to help yourself and your relationship by working to transform bitterness into compassion and understanding. This step is about giving your partner the benefit of the doubt. You acknowledge your partner's flaws but still strive to see his or her good intentions. You want to be able to disagree with your partner with love. You will see that as you become more forgiving, there is simultaneously less to be upset with. When you disagree forgivingly, you disagree as friends, not as enemies.

Marriage is unique among our close family relationships in that, unlike our parents or our siblings, we choose our partner. In a committed relationship, each partner shares the responsibility to make the relationship work. In the family, the parents have more responsibility for the health of the overall family relationship than the children do. The parents are older, have more life experience, and are the ones who chose to have children in the first place. There is also a natural order between siblings: generally the older brothers and sisters have greater power or say in the family, and it often stays that way for life. However, when lovers decide to become a couple, they start as equals. It is understood that they will share the effort it takes to create a successful relationship and that each will try to bring commitment, loyalty, patience, forgiveness, and follow-through to that effort.

When we commit to our lovers, we implicitly promise to forgive them. There is no other way we can live with someone for better or worse or until death do us part. However, relationships can founder when this contract to forgive is not understood and followed by both partners. Good relationships are precious, and all relationships are difficult to maintain, so we forgive our partner because of the love we feel and our desire to sustain the relationship. The dismal marriage statistics attest to how difficult it is to sustain an intimate partnership and prove that good relationships require effort and hard work. Over time people forget to appreciate each other, and their bad qualities emerge. Forgiveness is built around the idea that we do not have to escalate feelings of hurt and disappointment into outrage or depression. One way we can avoid doing this is by choosing to see our lovers in the best possible light. We can choose to interpret their behavior in ways that maintain their dignity, and we can empathize with our partners instead of demonizing them. We make an agreement with ourselves to look at our partners, as much as possible, through the eyes of love. The eyes of love reveal our partners to be wounded individuals who make mistakes, not terrible people trying to do harm.

In a way you are giving your partner a break by not taking his or her bad behavior personally. You understand that your partner is not usually trying to hurt you and that whatever your partner does is guided by his or her own wounds and needs. You are better able to give your partner a break when you can soothe yourself when you feel hurt and thereby not be as reactive and hostile to your partner. You can soothe yourself in part by practicing PERT (Positive Emotion Refocusing Technique), a technique I'll discuss in more detail later in the chapter, as well as the mind-body meditations from the previous chapter. There will always be times when you need soothing because no matter how good your marriage is, you are in a relationship with someone who is very different from you, in ways both trivial and important.

One of the difficult tasks of any successful marriage is to get to know your lover as a person in his or her own right rather than as just one half of your relationship. Even after we get to know our lovers, it can be a difficult task to accept them for their differences as well as their similarities. When you accept and forgive your partner, you can challenge your partner's weaknesses with love and understanding. You can be your partner's friend, rather than an enemy, even in an argument. Accepting your partner's differences and problematic qualities is at the heart of friendship and is a difficult passage for many couples.

It is incredibly important, and critical to any thriving marriage, that spouses see each other as separate persons with unique goals and desires. This is not easy to do. In the first thrall of love, people tend to look for and find their similarities with each other and to ignore obvious differences. It's normal to see the ways a new partner thinks like us and to focus on the things that bind us together. When you talk to people in the "honeymoon" phase of a relationship, they often gush about how much alike they are and how much they see things the same way. In fact, a couple in the first stages of love will go to great lengths to find similarities with each other, even if none are apparent to other people.

New couples do this for good reason. When we first join with another person, we want to know that our partners have enough similar traits and experiences that they are likely to stay around. We need to feel confident that we share the same goals and interests in life. It's also important to feel that our partners share our moral values and agree with us on what is normal and good. Honoring shared experiences and values is a cornerstone of a couple's joint identity.

After a while a new couple realizes that for all their similarities they are still different in significant ways. For many couples, this is a problematic stage, and it requires a good deal of forgiveness. Tom and Judy were a young couple who had many important and obvious similarities. Both were very physical and athletic, neither wanted children, and both worked as teachers. They had similar senses of humor and were raised by families who lived only an hour apart. In addition, Tom and Judy were both lapsed Catholics with a strong sense of spirituality. From the beginning, they found it easy to talk and share their feelings, and they felt blessed to have found each other. They agreed on the size of the house they wanted and the neighborhood they wanted to live in. However, as time went by and the honeymoon phase wore off, they found that they had one major difference. As Tom and Judy struggled to deal with this difference, they were hampered by the fact that both of them felt that their way of doing things was right and proper, and neither was interested in changing.

The problem was a simple one: Tom was a morning person, and Judy was not. Tom would shoot out of bed to start in on a long list of things to accomplish immediately, while Judy tended to get started more slowly, sipping her coffee and gradually gathering steam. When Judy had first fallen in love with Tom, she sacrificed her normal rhythm for the good of the relationship. As they grew more used to each other, Judy returned to her regular, slower morning rhythm. To their mutual chagrin, problems started to emerge now that they were no longer perfectly in synch.

Tom and Judy also discovered that Judy wanted quick closure after an argument, while Tom wanted some time to think things through. She felt that it was important to find common ground quickly, while Tom had to first fully understand his point of view. This created conflict and hurt feelings in both parties. Over time Tom and Judy also learned that they had greater differences in sexual desire than they had seen at first blush. This caused no end of struggle and pain.

Tom and Judy were a normal couple. The difficulties they faced were common and happen in every relationship. There was nothing unusual in having differing sexual needs and different schedules. Neither partner was wrong or right, but the ongoing health of their relationship depended on how they navigated their differences. Both Tom and Judy felt betrayed when their problems first surfaced. Each of them wondered what had happened to their great relationship and agreeable partner. Both felt confused by the sudden disagreement because they had grown to expect acceptance and shared desires from their partner. Tom and Judy had both hoped that this relationship would be the first in their lives to be conflict-free. Now that there was conflict, they struggled to understand it. Did the conflict mean that they had made a mistake or that they had somehow lied to each other?

Eventually Tom and Judy were able to save and strengthen their relationship. They did this by following the steps I've already presented and by working very hard to be each other's friend. They accepted that they had freely chosen each other and that all people have flaws. Although Tom and Judy understood how to appreciate each other, they were still stuck. They had not yet grasped the importance of knowing their partner's weaknesses and handling them with friendship and love. It took some effort, but eventually they were able to understand and respect each other's idiosyncrasies. Instead of being frustrated that Judy wanted closure so quickly, Tom came to see that it arose from a deep desire for harmony in their relationship. For her part, Judy was able to see that Tom was actually being very wise when he strove to understand his own feelings before making peace with her. Tom and Judy were able to come together as a couple and see the benefit in their different schedules, with one having lots of energy in the morning and the other having the stamina to make it to the end of the day. Ultimately, Tom and Judy were able to solve their problems by being each other's friend. Research shows that friendship is at the heart of successful relationships.

The next step in the process of forgiveness is deepening core aspects of your friendship with your partner.

It is important to increase the friendship you show your partner for two reasons. First, it is much easier to forgive a friend, because a friend is someone whose behavior you understand. After a few years of friendship, you will have experienced your partner's thinking and behavior, and it will be less threatening to you. Another important reason to deepen your friendship with your lover is that you are more likely to be kind and loving toward someone you consider a friend. Friendship is an invitation to be kind and generous to both ourselves and our partners. When your lover is your friend, you understand that he or she was not put on earth just to make you happy. Your lover has as much right as you do to have personal habits and quirks. When we are truly friends with our partners, we show them goodwill and do not just expect to have goodwill shown to us.

The next two aspects of friendship are important to understand as we move forward in the forgiveness process. First, it's important to encourage your partner to talk with you about anything and everything so that you can learn as much as you can about your partner. Second, you want to use what you learn to see your partner's actions in the kindest and most generous and understanding light you can. Many of you reading this book have already figured out how to listen well to your partner. The important step for you is to use what you know about your partner to keep the love connection strong, even when you do not like your partner's actions.

Unfortunately, research shows that many of us do not spend enough time talking and listening to our partners. One study claimed that married couples typically have twenty-eight minutes of face-to-face communication with each other a week. Another showed that a majority of married people could not pick out the gift their husband or wife would most want. The important thing here is to accept how important it is to listen to your partner so that you can understand, love, and forgive him or her when necessary. The kind of things we need to be able to talk to our partners about include how they were raised, their relationship to their families, and the problems they had growing up. While your partner is speaking, try to see things the way he or she sees them. Try to understand all the ways in which your lover was both wounded and encouraged. You aren't just looking for information about how your lover was screwed up—you are trying to develop a clear picture of the person you are with. Then you can use that clear picture to be as kind and empathic as possible.

As you talk further, you can ask your partner about past lovers and try to find out the details of what worked and what didn't in those relationships. Again, you want to be able to see things the way your lover sees them. You want to be able to see the ways your lover was hurt and understand what your lover learned from the experience. You are not looking at your partner's old relationships for comparison purposes, but to help you understand the

pain he or she felt and may still feel. You might ask your husband
to open up about how he spent his day and what stresses he faced.
Try to understand the struggles in his life and the challenges he
faces. Be sensitive to whether your wife is having a stressful time at
work or dealing with issues with her family or friends. Being sensitive means that you are fully aware of the strain she is under and
you relate to her with support and understanding. When you act
as your lover's friend, you are following the golden rule: you are
offering your lover the understanding and support you hope he or
she would provide you.

There are many ways in which to continue this communication with your loved one. Try talking about the things your lover
likes and dislikes, or what causes your lover pleasure or pain. If
you don't already know them, discuss your lover's goals and
deepest wishes. While you are having these talks, make sure you
are aware of what makes your partner special and make it clear
that you intend to check in like this on a regular basis.

By being present for our partners, we help them with their
frustrations and sense of alienation when their life is off track.
We are also better able to celebrate with our lovers when things
are in alignment. The point is that it is vital to take an ongoing
and active interest in our lovers' lives and not simply expect them
to be interested in us. When we watch our lovers' actions, we
can learn about them. When we talk with our lovers and listen
to them, we can understand how they think. This kind of friendship and understanding is predicated on the fact that our lovers
do not have to act the way we do and do not need our approval
for how they live their lives.

So many of the habits we bring to our marriages originated in
childhood. Our lovers' personalities are a combination of their
basic temperament, which is largely genetic, and environmental
influences, which were strongest when they were young. Our

partners grew up in homes with their own sets of rules, and they had unique experiences there. Their sense of what is "normal" and how they react to us are largely based on these childhood experiences. The more we can understand our lovers' past, the easier it is to make sense out of their current behavior. Understanding their history often helps us to see our differences without taking them personally. This in turn makes us less reactive, more centered, and therefore better able to talk things out.

Understanding your loved one's behavior is a necessary midpoint of the forgiveness exercise, but it is not the endpoint. Finding a gentle and generous way to comprehend your partner's life experience, so that you stay connected and on the same side even when you disagree, is the endpoint. Toby and Jane were a married couple who struggled with these issues. Jane, an intelligent and attractive woman of thirty-five, was used to things going her way, and she had problems compromising. Her wealthy parents had spoiled their only child rotten; as an adult, she was willful and headstrong and did not negotiate well. Jane was exciting and dynamic and a good deal of fun—when things were going her way. Toby loved his wife, and the relationship was solid for several years, even though Jane required a good deal of attention and forbearance.

The careful balance in their relationship was threatened when Jane gave birth to their first child. She was unable to balance the demands of her baby and her husband. Toby was committed to his marriage and child and made the effort to work things out. The first thing he had to understand in counseling was that Jane's behavior was "normal," given her childhood, and that it would have been silly to expect her to act in any other way. Toby was wise enough to realize that Jane was not trying to be unkind—she had simply never learned the rules of the give-and-take of adult relationships. He was also finally able to see that Jane was not a happy woman. Jane's inflexibility and her desperate need for things to go her way made her life very difficult; she suffered from her inability to be successful as both a wife and a mother. Toby's insights allowed him to continue to love his wife but also compelled him to take a stand. That stand was relatively gentle: all Toby asked was that Jane be as willing to work on the relationship as he was.

Toby and Jane's relationship shows that being empathic and generous does not mean that you have to be a doormat or that your partner can get away with bad behavior. It was good for Janet to understand that the experience of being beaten as a child had taught her husband Charlie to be physically violent when stressed. It was not good to stay and allow Charlie to beat her up in turn. However, understanding where Charlie learned his behavior helped to make it less personal for Janet and allowed her to be less defensive when talking with him. It was good for Toni to understand that Marvin's problems with commitment stemmed from his alcoholic, untrustworthy parents. Remaining with Marvin while he cheated on her wasn't so good.

Friendship, kindness, and goodwill are important, but you must recognize the difference between being compassionate and kind toward your partner and simply cooperating with poor behavior. You do not want to enable deliberately unkind or abusive behavior. In those situations, your safety comes first; once you're safe, you can concern yourself with forgiveness. The ultimate goal is to be your partner's loving friend so that you can forgive him or her for problematic traits and at the same time ensure that you take good care of yourself and any children.

It was one thing for Jeff to understand that Cynthia was raised to fear and repress her sexuality, and another for him to accept her discomfort with sex for the duration of their marriage. A loving understanding of Cynthia's past history and current confusion could make the sexual negotiation in their relationship more fruitful. If Jeff could accept that this was a problem Cynthia had dealt with in all of her relationships—not just with him—he could be gentler with her. When he could see Cynthia as someone who struggled with intimacy, he could talk to her with more compassion, patience, and kindness. It was up to him whether he dealt with Cynthia as a friend or an enemy. He could choose to focus only on his own needs or on a mixture of his needs and her struggle.

The more understanding we have for our lovers when we discuss relationship problems, the less defensive they need to be. Cynthia would probably have preferred to be a more sexually responsive woman. It is highly unlikely that she wanted to trigger such difficulty in her relationships. However, her life experience had made sexual ease quite difficult, while Jeff preferred a more sexually available partner. His problem was that the woman he chose could not easily provide what he wanted. His challenge was to remain kind and supportive while helping Cynthia grow if she wanted to.

This fourth step toward forgiveness requires a willingness on your part to uncover the good in your partner. Some of your problems with your partner are probably caused by good intentions gone bad. As the saying goes, "The road to hell is paved with good intentions." Most likely, your lover wants to do the right thing but sometimes is not capable of it. Your partner means well but is not skillful at fulfilling his or her good intentions. John wanted to be a good listener for his wife Jan, but whenever she criticized him, he tuned her out. He had learned the tuning-out mechanism to help him deal with his father's incessant criticism. Jan struggled to balance John's obvious desire to be a loving partner with his poor listening habits and past family history that made his behavior inevitable. Both Jan and John were frustrated by John's desire to communicate effectively with his wife but his inability to do so.

We make things worse when we focus on our partners' failings and ignore their good intentions and understandable weaknesses. Jerome and Kelley struggled over the different ways they parented their children. Jerome got annoyed over the amount of time Kelley spent with their kids, and it frustrated him that she thought about them all the time. Kelley's passion for their children and lack of interest in their marriage made him feel neglected. Jerome expressed himself by being snide and pissed off around her. For her part, Kelley thought that Jerome lacked parenting skills and was self-centered and childish. Kelley felt that Jerome did not understand the effort required to raise a couple of kids and work at a job. As far as she was concerned, Jerome minimized the enormous effort she was putting into raising the children. Kelley felt unappreciated and raw and started to avoid spending time with him whenever she could.

It was only when Jerome and Kelley took forgiveness training that they finally started to appreciate each other. They practiced deep belly breathing when upset, and both learned to see the good underlying the other's actions. Jerome understood that Kelley was not trying to reject him—she simply wanted to make the best home possible for her children. He saw how deeply committed she was to her family and how much she was willing to sacrifice. He realized that Kelley was working long, hard hours on minimal sleep. At some level, he understood that she was willing to sacrifice a bit of her happiness with him to properly launch their children. Jerome finally started to see that his wife's behavior was driven by her dogged determination and love for both him and the kids. Kelley was also able to finally see that Jerry was not just lazy but deeply committed to their well-being as a couple. She realized that he was making significant efforts to strengthen their bond as a married couple, but that he also just wanted to spend more time with her. She began to respond to his love and not just to the rejection of her parenting.

We need to be both friend and lover to our spouses so that we can fully see all the good qualities in them. Once we start to look underneath our partners' actions and words, we can find their good intentions and their often frustrated attempt to love. As we learn to celebrate their goodness, we are able to offer them kindness and compassion in return, and yet we remain free to disagree with some of the manifestations of our lovers' intentions. Jerome could appreciate the deep love Kelley had for their children and acknowledge her willingness to work hard. However, he could still say that in his opinion she was spending too much time caring for the kids and not enough time with him. He could recognize her goodness and still disagree with her actions. In that way, he forgave her, yet was calm and loving enough to have a productive conversation with her. Kelley could see Jerome's attention to her in the loving light in which it was intended and still tell him there was not enough time in the day to get everything done. She could believe that Jerome needed to be a more involved and active parent and still treat her husband with respect and kindness. Kelley learned to honor the good in Jerome while maintaining her ability to push back when needed.

As you go along the path of forgiveness, it is important to retain your ability to criticize and draw limits with your partner. However, as we connect with our lovers' goodness or deeply understand their pain or motivation, we often lose the desire to call their behavior "wrong." Even more profoundly, as we connect with the compassion and forgiveness within us, we lose our desire to hurt our lovers. I have heard countless stories of people who dropped their grudges once they started to understand their partner. A wife can forgive a husband with poor communication skills once she sees that he is really trying to connect. Seeing the effort he is making opens her heart to him, and she becomes more patient and accepting. Suzie forgave Jim for his frequent work trips once she was able to see how desperately he loved their kids. Tammie forgave her husband once she was able to lovingly realize how hard it was for him to express his feelings.

I have taught countless couples to understand that they can both want what is best for their children and still disagree on specific methods. They can agree that their children's interests come first, but disagree on what that means. They both want what is best for their children, so there is no right or wrong, just a negotiation to figure out a compromise. By forgiving first and negotiating second, a couple can disagree yet still forgive each other. Other couples learn that they can agree on wanting a strong marriage, yet disagree on the methods they might use to get there. Again, it is best for the couple to forgive first and negotiate second. When couples are joined in commitment and respect for each other's good intentions, they can forget about who is "right and who is wrong" and just work on resolving their problems.

When we approach our lovers with friendship and forgiveness, we are able to use what we know about our lovers to see how their behaviors make sense. Our knowledge of our lovers' history and needs allows us to understand their thoughts and motivations. Once we can understand this, we may disagree with our lovers, but we will rarely hate them. Approaching our relationships with forgiveness and friendship forces us to understand that our lovers always do the best they can, but unfortunately their best is sometimes not very good. Human nature is such that we all fail to live up to our potential at times. When we understand that our loved ones tried and failed, that understanding allows us to love the sinner and hate the sin. We can be angry about something our lovers did without casting them from our hearts. If we can clearly see our lovers' struggles and pain, we will be able to look compassionately at how they lead their lives.

The most important thing to do is to connect deeply with your lover's good intentions so that you can forgive your lover's failed manifestations of those intentions. Ultimately you want to provide your loved one with every chance to change for the better and grow in skill. What you want to see is the goodness that underlies your lover's behavior. If you can hold on to that, then it becomes easier to acknowledge, without bitterness, how poorly your lover has carried out his or her good intentions. The ultimate goal is to be able to offer compassion and understanding to your lover while disagreeing with his or her choices.

In this step of forgiveness and friendship, you are managing your own frustration and reactivity for the good of your health and the health of your relationship. By controlling your reactions to your lover, you manage to control some of the blame and anger you might otherwise feel. When you learn to soothe your own mentally or emotionally distressed self, you no longer have to rely on your partner to soothe you. In this regard it is particularly helpful to practice the Positive Emotion Refocusing Technique (PERT) on a regular basis. Practicing PERT is helpful not only when you are upset with your lover but in particular when you need to find a kinder way to look at his or her behavior and thinking. PERT is a simple practice that puts you in touch with your own goodness so that you can find it in your lover.

PERT practice is an example of the interaction of your mind and body. As you quiet your body, your mind calms down as well. It is important when you practice to breathe slowly and deeply and to bring your attention to your stomach. It is also good to be careful when you choose a positive image: if you are really upset with your lover, find someone else to think of, because the point is to create a loving experience. On the other hand, when you are disconnected from your lover but not angry or resentful, it is good to picture your lover when practicing PERT. Try to see your lover in the most delicious way possible so that you can really reconnect with your love.

PERT (Positive Emotion Refocusing Technique)

When you are feeling the effects of an unresolved grievance or problem with your lover in your mind or your body:

1. Bring your attention to your stomach as you slowly draw two slow, deep breaths in and out.

2. As you inhale, allow the air to gently push your belly out. As you exhale, consciously relax your belly so that it feels "soft."

3. On the third full and deep inhalation, bring to your mind's eye an image of someone you love (but are not currently upset with) or of a beautiful scene in nature that fills you with awe and peace.

4. Visualize first and then try to feel in your body the love or awe you have. It is optimal to center these feelings in the area around your heart.

5. While practicing this visualization, continue with slow and *soft* belly breathing.

Practicing PERT when you are upset with your lover will gradually reduce the power he or she has to disturb your peace. You will experience some peace with your first practice, and therefore you will feel a little safer. Practicing PERT when you are with your partner will make it easier for you to talk with him or her. If you practice when you are alone, you gain confidence and strengthen your ability to stay cool in dealing with your lover in stressful situations.

I also recommend PERT as a way to find alternative ways of thinking or behaving about the problems you face with your lover. You can practice PERT when you want to find a more loving and kinder way to think about your partner. To get this level of change in your relationship, it is helpful to add step six to your practice of PERT. You want to add step six to the first five steps after you have practiced steps one through five a number of times.

6. After you are calm and peaceful, ask the gentler part of yourself that is centered in your heart what you can do or think to be more loving and understanding toward your partner.

PERT practice will be helpful in any situation in which you feel anger, hurt, depression, or bitterness toward your lover. My students practice PERT when they remember how an ex-spouse or current lover mistreated them. They also practice PERT when they find themselves getting upset in an ongoing marital struggle. PERT takes about forty-five seconds to practice and can be done anytime and anywhere. No one has to know you are practicing PERT. You can practice in an argument with your lover today and learn to stay cool. You can practice while your partner is telling you something you do not want to hear. You can practice when you need to be assertive and are worried about your partner's reaction. You can practice when you are stuck and want to feel more love for your partner.

PERT is the most powerful technique I know to help you remain in control of your emotions and manage your stress. Practicing PERT helps you stay calm so that you can make good decisions. The bottom line is that staying calm when confronted with a painful memory or current situation helps you avoid blaming someone for ruining your life. As you practice PERT, the pain your relationship causes you becomes less threatening and the good parts of the relationship become more apparent. You take away some of your lover's power to hurt you and replace it with increased self-confidence and calm.

I taught Cynthia the technique, and to her credit, she was open enough to try it. After all, practicing PERT was cheaper than the pint of ice cream she ate every day to soothe herself when she fought with Jeff about sex. Cynthia felt that she was going crazy from Jeff's insensitive demands to have sex every day. In her desperation, she began faithfully practicing PERT every day. At first all she noticed were the familiar feelings of anger and victimhood. We talked about the technique again and about the importance of keeping her attention on her belly—not on the emotional distress she was feeling—and deeply relaxing her body through breathing. With time, the positive emotions would come.

Cynthia practiced each day for two weeks. By the end of this period, she could think of her boyfriend without reacting like a puppet on a string. Through the practice of PERT, Cynthia gained control over her feelings and became more confident. She was also able to start thinking about what she wanted out of life. She realized that while she was afraid of Jeff's desire for her and frightened by her own sexual needs, she clearly wanted a successful relationship. She saw that she would need professional help to move on.

Cynthia also started to wonder why she was spending so much time simply reacting to Jeff's frustration and anger. When she thought about it, she realized that in some ways he was reacting normally to her severe sexual inhibition. He obviously loved her enough to stick around, but her inhibitions left him feeling hurt and rejected. Once Cynthia was able to see that Jeff's intentions were good, she was able to forgive his crude methods of communication that only made things worse. Before she started practicing PERT, Cynthia got upset every time she thought of Jeff or of sex. Now her nervous system was calm enough that she could feel empathy for her boyfriend and compassion toward herself. She forgave Jeff for his unskillful communication and his exaggerated reactions because she recognized his desire for her and commitment to their relationship. Cynthia was finally able to call Jeff on the rough, crude way he talked to her and demand that he stop. Cynthia also calmed down enough to acknowledge that she needed help, and they both started therapy, which was eventually successful.

What worked with Cynthia has worked with countless people. Cynthia connected with her goodness and was able to see more of it in Jeff. She saw Jeff's good intentions and also his unskillful execution of them. She also acknowledged that she could not heal on her own and she got help. But most of all, she practiced a powerful mind-body exercise that allowed her to feel stronger and more at peace and that gave her access to a loving part of herself that she had felt was lost.

◆

NINE

Step 5:
Accept What You Can't
Change and Grieve Your Loss

The concept of accepting what you can't change and grieving your loss is adapted from the serenity prayer, which is a core element of twelve-step programs. The adaptation discussed in this chapter is an affirmation of the acceptance element of that prayer. It exhorts us to accept what we cannot change and to change what we can. The affirmation reminds us that wisdom is the ability to discern the difference between the things we can and cannot change. Recognizing that difference saves us a great deal of heartache and wasted effort. We generally cannot change the actions and thoughts of other people or what happened in our own past. What we can change is ourselves. Forgiveness is one way to change ourselves and in that way change our relationships with our lovers. As we change, we go from anger and self-pity to understanding and goodwill. Becoming a more forgiving person helps us to change our focus from our wounds to the present and future possibilities for happiness in our marriage.

The use of the serenity prayer in twelve-step programs has been a balm both for substance abusers and for those who have lived with substance abusers. Part of the twelve-step process is accepting a higher power and changing your behavior for the better. The wisdom contained in the serenity prayer is useful to anyone in a long-term relationship, and it is particularly helpful for couples who are dealing with situations that are out of their control, such as chronic or terminal illness or a job that requires moving out of state. Any relationship will have difficult aspects that do not go away, no matter how much we dislike them, and painful memories from the past that do not change, no matter how much we want them to.

The serenity prayer tells you to change the things you can change and accept the things you can't change. You cannot change the fact that your wife had an affair or smashed the car. There is nothing you can do to change the reality that your husband is losing his hair or has diabetes. There may be things that you *can* change about your partner, and you should certainly do so when you can. You won't know if your partner will respond to your efforts unless you try. You might try encouraging your wife to pick up after herself, or letting your husband know the consequences of forgetting to pick the kids up from day care. I've advised some of my clients to work harder to make their lovers change. I told Tom to be more assertive with Louise over her forgetfulness. The crucial thing is for Tom to be as kind as possible, but not to let Louise off the hook for her errors. I did this because we both needed to know whether Louise could control her behavior or not.

We can approach our lovers from a place of forgiveness and still ask them to change or to help us if we need help. We can approach problems with our loved ones with the desire to try to make our relationships and lives better. This can be difficult when our partners know that we are not okay with their difficult tendencies and bad habits but they still refuse to change. The serenity prayer asks us to think about how much unhappiness we are willing to experience trying to change things we have no control over. The average age for first marriage in the United States now is between twenty-four and twenty-six, and there are multiple remarriages at all ages. This means that our partners had plenty of time to develop their personalities before we came on the scene. Our partners may not change a long-term disagreeable quality just because it bothers us or we find it wrong. The serenity prayer is so helpful precisely because none of us can change some of our lovers' most difficult traits.

Using the serenity prayer requires understanding and intelligence. You have to learn the difference between your lover's acceptable flaws and the flaws that are a spur to leave the relationship. Sometimes giving your partner all the friendship, appreciation, and benefit of the doubt you can still won't be enough to let you be at peace with something your partner does. Perhaps the problem is a onetime event, such as Laurie's affair with a coworker when Jack was sick. Or perhaps the problem is chronic, such as Kellie's terrible spending habits, which put her and her husband Cory close to bankruptcy.

Sometimes your partner will have tendencies that wear you down over time. Henry's wife Kristin was completely self-absorbed. There were times in their relationship when Henry was able to say to himself, "I chose Kristin, and I am at peace with her. Her self-absorption is the thorn on my rosebush, and I love this rose enough to live with the thorns." Henry accepted that Kristin's flaws were a part of who she was and that they wouldn't change even if she had a different spouse. He made a point to remember the many good things she brought to his life, and this helped him in many situations. Henry enjoyed Kristin's lively personality and dynamic intelligence. She was sexy and fun to be with. Finally, Henry was also able to develop a compassionate awareness of Kristin's upbringing, which made her self-absorption understandable. There were many times when he simply understood why she did what she did and accepted her behavior without resentment.

One day, however, Kristin did something that made Henry feel so angry and abandoned that he couldn't accept her behavior. His oldest and dearest friend had died, and during the funeral service Kristin was offended by something someone said. She was so caught up in her anger that she was unable to offer any support to Henry. All Henry wanted was to feel that Kristen was with him in his corner, but she was so lost in her petty dispute that he felt completely abandoned.

Henry was profoundly hurt by his wife's actions. He had to finally accept that there was an aspect to Kristin's personality that was truly toxic. Henry felt emotionally distressed and angry at the way she had behaved. All of us will experience times when our partners do something that for some reason or another overwhelms our ability to be understanding toward them and throws us for a loop. It could be the first time they do it or the thirtieth. For Henry, it was the vulnerability he felt at the funeral of his friend and his wife's inability to provide any support for his loss.

These kinds of behaviors are still forgivable, but you may have to utilize the fifth step in the forgiveness process to deal with them. The fifth step asks us to honestly accept that our partners did something truly bad before we try to forgive them. Then we acknowledge that we can't change that behavior and we become willing to experience the grief that ensues. Sometimes no matter how smartly you handle yourself or how kind you may be, things with your lover do not work out the way you hoped. Henry had always done his best to accept Kristin's behavior and prior to the funeral had held out hope that she might change.

There will come a time in your relationship when your lover hurts you and you have to grieve the wound. Perhaps your spouse has an affair, or you may simply be hurt by a fundamental difference in beliefs or habits. Experiencing such pain does not mean there is anything wrong with you or the relationship. But it does prompt you to acknowledge that some relationships can't be fixed and may not work out. When you lose your sense of safety in your relationship, you may just have to suck it up and move on. If your spouse abuses drugs or has an affair or simply refuses to use good parenting practices, you may have to accept that it is time to leave the relationship. A period of pain and anger will follow as you deal with the loss. This period is commonly called "grieving," and it's an important part of the process of forgiveness.

It is normal to experience emotional distress when our world is shaken. It is also human nature to grieve losses and to suffer when we are mistreated. The situations that trigger emotional distress will be different for everyone, and some people will fall apart more readily than others. There are some universally distressing experiences, such as coming home and seeing our lover in bed with someone else, and there are others that are more idiosyncratic, such as how we react when our partner puts a dent in the car. People's reactions to the same experience differ widely: some suffer for a few moments, while others may be hurt for a few months.

Every time you disagree with or are hurt by your lover, you must acknowledge the pain you are dealing with. Most of the time the pain will last only for a moment, and then you can remember why you love your partner, come up with a benign explanation, and get over it. In those situations, the grief response can be very quick. Your gut will suddenly feel tight, or there will be a swear word on your lips. However, after a few moments of grateful thinking or practicing PERT, it is over. With practice, you can increase the number of situations you can successfully handle in this way, and you will feel more confident in yourself and your relationship.

Some of your losses are small, such as accepting that your lover will never like football the way you do. There may be grief in that loss, a coming to terms with the fact that something you love will not be shared with your partner. Other losses are huge, like grappling with the knowledge that your lover may never be sober. For many difficulties we can simply use one of the four steps I have already discussed and through simple practice experience goodwill toward our partners. Not all difficulties, however, are ones that we can move through without an active and extended time of grieving. The period of grief begins when we fully embrace the reality that there is a painful experience in our relationship that we do not want and we cannot change. We accept our inability to make a change, and this acceptance allows us to then feel the sadness, anger, and fear that come with loss.

An ability to grieve appropriately is a necessary part of a successful marriage, but many couples do not realize this. Grief is the normal response of the mind and body to loss and is biologically programmed into human beings. The death of a parent or our partner causes a deep ache that we do not get over quickly. When our partner cheats or shatters our innocence with a betrayal, the devastation can last for a long time. Sometimes normal grief can take up to two years to run its course. A process I developed to help people through their grieving in their relationship is called the HEAL method. You can think of HEAL as an advanced form of PERT practice.

HEAL starts with a long version of PERT, similar to the "appreciative breathing" from chapter 7. Practicing HEAL can release long-suffering wounds. After a few practices, it can restore peace to those who have had experiences so painful that recovery seemed impossible. Like PERT, HEAL can be practiced quickly—in less than a minute—to deal with a specific hurt, but you will need ten to fifteen minutes to be successful with the longer version. The HEAL method is designed for use after you have learned and practiced the major tenets of my forgiveness method. It is not simply an add-on but a powerful way to reinforce and practice my forgiveness process.

The HEAL method was instrumental in helping Sandra move through substantial grief. Sandra, now in her midsixties, had endured a long and difficult marriage to a workaholic husband, Eric. Eric had been very successful in business but was absent from home a great deal. On those rare occasions when he was home, he was usually working or tired and had little energy for Sandra. Eric promised that when he retired things would be different and the two of them would finally do things together.

Eric retired when he was sixty-five and was miserable for the first year of his retirement. He missed his work, had few friends, and was lost without an office to go to. After twelve months, however, his depression and irritability lifted, his mood improved, and he and Sandra became closer than at any other time in their marriage. Sandra was happily anticipating getting to really know her husband when he fell ill. Eric had felt sick and dizzy after a long day of golf, and when his symptoms didn't improve, Sandra drove him to the hospital, where they found out he'd had a stroke. Although Eric wasn't crippled by the strokes, both he and Sandra were deeply affected by them. Eric lost some of his memory, suffered impaired speech, and was often moody and easily fatigued.

Sandra felt that the time they spent happy together had been a bitter tease. She was just getting used to having a husband when he was taken from her again. Sandra came to my forgiveness class because a year and a half after the stroke she was still mad at her husband for having waited so long to join his life with hers. She felt cheated out of their time together and frustrated by her years of waiting. Sandra had to make peace with the reality of her situation, so we spent time on the serenity prayer in class. Sandra also had the very difficult task of grieving so much of her married life. She had longed for a close and loving partnership her whole life but had experienced it for only a short period. For the first thirty years of their life together, Eric had refused to help her create a close and joined partnership. For most of that time, Eric and Sandra had been on parallel tracks. It was only when Eric got sick that they came together in the same place at the same time.

Each letter of HEAL corresponds to one aspect of the grief and forgiveness process: Hope, Educate, Affirm, and Long-term. I describe each aspect separately in the following section, but the steps are combined when we practice the HEAL method.

H Is for Hope

The first component of HEAL is to make a strong statement of Hope—what I call an H statement. The H statement represents the specific positive outcome that you hope for when your partner has hurt you, such as wanting love or time or sex or a clean house. Simone was consumed by memories of a love affair that went bad. By learning to say, "I wanted my relationship with Clark to be a long and loving partnership," she kept her goal in focus. Before this practice, Simone was not thinking of what she had wanted because she was obsessed with what she had lost. The H in HEAL helped her remember what it was that she would have liked to see happen.

I chose the word "hope" carefully and deliberately. People often confuse what they *hope* will happen with what *has* to happen. This confusion results in the creation of unenforceable rules, as discussed in chapter 6. Unenforceable rules are at the root of our suffering and create the soil in which grievances can grow. When we create an H statement, we are reminding ourselves that we wished or hoped for something to go our way. We hoped to be loved, to have an equal coparent, or to get along with our in-laws. We hoped to be safe in our home, to have a faithful spouse, or to have our partner treat us with respect and honesty.

Making H statements is a way to remind ourselves of the goal that lies just under the hurt. Telling ourselves that all we can ever do is *hope* things go our way is a good reminder to accept but not to be defeated by life's uncertainty. Asserting our hopes is a statement of health and power once we understand that not all our hopes will come true. There is a vulnerability in hoping for things; assertion and power come from accepting this. By coupling assertion and power with our vulnerability, we make a commitment to not be prevented from strongly hoping for good things to happen. With this approach, we make every reasonable effort to get our hopes realized.

The H statement must be worded in positive terms. Your hope should be expressed in terms of what you wanted to *happen*, not what you wanted to *avoid*. It is often difficult to make positive H statements. A lot of people find it difficult not to say that they wanted bad things to not have happened to them. They have a hard time remembering they once wanted something good. Saying, "I wanted my husband not to cheat on me," is not the same as saying, "I wanted a strong and faithful marriage." The first response is worded negatively, the second positively. Before she practiced HEAL, Simone would say, "I hoped that he would not leave me." However, that was not really what she had hoped for: her real hope was for a stable and loving relationship. The H statement can take some work as you remember the positive hope that lay under your desire for something bad not to have happened.

The second condition for a successful H statement is making it personal. You are making an H statement for yourself, not for anyone else. To do this you must make an assertive statement of your goal, not just express a general wish that something good will happen. In an H statement, you are not just wishing for happiness but hoping to achieve a specific personal goal. You are wishing not just for a good relationship but for love with a particular person. To this end, the H statement usually begins with the word "I," and the focus is on your specific goal.

Finally, besides being phrased in positive terms and reflecting a personal goal, your H statement should also reflect your specific hope. Don't make your H statement too general. A good H statement would be something like, "I hoped Jim would be honest about his relationship with Susan." Statements like "I prefer that my relationship be pleasant" or "I wanted to marry an honest partner" are not good H statements. If you are addressing a marriage that has been destroyed by infidelity, then your H statement should concern that specific relationship, not relationships in general. When you are upset over an uncaring partner, you want to refer to the specific quality you want your partner to develop.

The H in HEAL is not about changing your lover's character. First of all, changing someone's personality is practically impossible. We cannot change other people unless they choose to change themselves. This confusion is at the root of most grievances. Many of us spend years uselessly trying to make our loved ones change. We get upset when our lovers do not agree to change for us. Forgiveness can resolve this upset and help us stop wasting our time trying to change partners who do not want to change.

A second problem emerges when we craft H statements about our lover's character. It is impossible to forgive something as abstract as a person's character, temperament, or personality. Our spouse's nature is too big a concept and too uncertain. At best we can forgive specific behavioral omissions or choices that may reflect his or her character. This important distinction can save us a lot of pain. We can see specific instances of behavior, but we can only hypothesize about character. Tilting at character windmills is not the best way to spend our limited resources of energy and time.

When criticizing your lover's character, remember that even married people spend plenty of time away from each other and you do not know how your spouse behaves out of your sight. Some people might be loving parents but lousy partners. Others could be poor parents and fantastic spouses. Some people are wonderful with casual friends but struggle with deep emotional intimacy. It's also possible that your lover is great with people he or she knows but unskillful at communicating with casual acquaintances. When we try to generalize about character beyond the behavior we have observed, we run the risk of being wrong. To forgive, you need to focus on specific behaviors—such as harsh speech or unkind action—that were at odds with what you wanted. Hoping that your husband might become nicer does not provide enough detail about the hoped-for behavior. A more specific hope—such as the hope that your husband would speak to you with tenderness after you visited your parents—is more helpful.

Please remember that there are no perfect H statements, but also that creating them is not rocket science. There is wiggle room for you when you create them. Your task is to think of exactly what you want that your lover does not provide. Phrase your H statement in positive terms, make it personal, and be as specific as you can. Keep the vague generalizations about your lover's character to a minimum, and above all be patient with yourself as you learn how to do this.

E Is for Educate

The E in HEAL stands for Educate. Your E statement will remind you that *there are limits to your control over your partner and yourself.* This statement acknowledges that you understand that you can have a specific hope but that you might not get what you want. It also reflects your realization that your hope may come out better than, worse than, or exactly how you anticipated it would. You do not know whether you will get what you want. Therefore, you hope, do your best, and await the results.

When we forget that all we can really do is hope or wish for the results we want, we make things harder for ourselves. When we forget that our ability to make our wishes come true is limited, we create grievances. Many people need to forgive soured relationships. Others are dealing with long-term marriages and love affairs that limp on, crippled by infidelity and barely suppressed anger. Some have simply been abandoned by those they love, while others live with a cruel and harsh partner. A common grievance is that a relationship ended before one partner was ready, or that the relationship continues, but in conflict and discord.

The E statement both acknowledges and fully accepts the possibility of not getting what you want. An appropriate E statement for Alice would reflect the inherent instability in all relationships. Her E statement could be something like: "Even though I really wanted the relationship with Gerry to work, I accept the fact that not all relationships succeed." While H statements get us in touch with our legitimate desire for a positive outcome, E statements remind us that there are always forces that resist our control. The good news is that, with practice, we can see our unenforceable rules melt away in the presence of a realistic outlook. As this happens, our grief will slowly soften and become easier to deal with.

The H statement is a personal statement of a wish or desire. The E statement acknowledges the impersonal possibility that we will not get what we want. We focus on the personal in H statements and on the impersonal in E statements. The best E statement reflects a personal desire yet accepts factors that are beyond our control. E statements are helpful because when we generalize about the cause of a wound, we take some of the personal sting away.

Alice's first attempt to construct an E statement was, "I will never find a good man, and I just have to live with it." This is a statement of self-pity, not an acceptance of realities that might help her heal. Like Alice, people generally have two difficulties when they try to craft E statements. The first mistake is to do what Alice did and confuse uncertainty with negative certainty. Alice did not know that she would never find a good man; she only knew that her last attempt had failed. There is a world of difference between negative certainty and uncertainty, and it is also the difference between healing and depression.

The experience of failing in love had made Alice want to give up hoping for a good relationship in the future. She chose hopelessness rather than the uncertainty of trying to make a new relationship work. Alice, in her hurt and confusion, thought she was accepting "reality." In fact, she was constructing her own idea of reality, in the same way that we create our dreams at night. She was also mistaking conjecture for fact: there is no certainty in committed relationships. Some relationships work, and some do not. Some people remain married until death, and others divorce in six months. Some long-term marriages are rich and intimate, and others are a living hell. Neither a good nor a bad certainty exists. I helped Alice to change her E statement to "I accept that many love affairs do not work out."

The second difficulty people have when crafting E statements is in accepting a certain degree of uncertainty. Try saying, "I understand and accept that...." Not all people are willing to do this, and some find the word "accept" too strong. If you agree, use the word "understand" instead; after all, there is not too much difference between "accept" and "understand." And try to remember one thing: you risk disappointment every time you want something from your partner. So much of forgiveness training involves accepting this simple fact of life.

An E statement has two parts. The first part is a general statement acknowledging that every hope carries with it the possibility of failure. Your lover may be disloyal, your relationship may end, your partner may be a bad parent, your lover may not be able to return your emotion. In the second part of the E statement, you accept the uncertainty of the first part. Your E statement does not condone any specific hurtful action; you can disagree with what your husband did yet still understand that his behavior was commonplace and you cannot control his behavior. What you are saying with the E statement is that you accept that hurtful things are a part of the vulnerability inherent in hoping for a good relationship with your lover.

Sandra's E statement focused on the possibility that the people we love might become ill. It was too hard for her to say that she accepted that uncertainty, but she was willing to say that she understood it. Sandra's H and E statements were: "I hoped to finally have some loving years with Eric after years of not really being that connected as a couple. However, I understand that even with the best of intentions, people become ill."

The H and E statements are the parts of the HEAL method that can cause feelings of sadness and loss. They focus on past experiences of something going wrong. By clearly articulating your hope, you are acknowledging that something you wanted did not happen. For some people, this statement intensifies their feelings of loss and sadness. The closer people get to their pain, the more likely they are to feel sadness. However, feelings of sadness are not inevitable when you practice the HEAL method.

There is nothing wrong with feeling sad. Sadness is a natural response to loss, and we all feel sad when we lose something important. Losing a dream is also an important loss. When a dream shatters, be it a dream of a joyful love affair, a loyal partner, or a dependable relationship or friendship, it can be very painful. Sadness is not the same as depression or hopelessness, which usually emerge from holding unenforceable rules. You are unlikely to feel despair simply from admitting that you were unable to get something you wanted and you are in pain. Some kinds of E statements, however, can cause depressive feelings. Alice, for instance, first responded to her failed relationship by asserting that she would never again have a good relationship.

Start practicing the HEAL method with a minute or two of deep belly breathing. Then bring your awareness to the area around your heart and think of something you love or are thankful for. As you do this, continue to breathe slowly and deeply into and out of your stomach. Then craft an appropriate H statement. This statement should be positive, personal, and specific. Release the H statement into the impersonality of the E statement. Remember to breathe slowly and deeply into and out of your belly, and keep your attention in your open heart.

The E statement acknowledges the uncertainty inherent in wanting anything. Attach the E statement to the end of the H statement. The two statements are best joined with the words "however" and "I understand and accept...." Practice the "hope" and "educate" parts of this process until you are comfortable with your statements.

The first two stages of the HEAL method focus on what caused your wound in the past. The H and E statements help orient your pain and loss and allow you to put them into a healing perspective. When you have practiced the H and E components a couple of times, you are ready to learn the A and L components of the HEAL method.

There is one more thing to discuss, however, before we go on to the next two components. Some people find it difficult to let go of their hurts and struggle to get from the E of the HEAL method to the A. The truth is that they are stuck in a rut with their way of thinking, and this causes them to repeatedly upset themselves. After practicing the H and the E of the HEAL method, Anita felt too sad to continue. As soon as she thought of her husband, she felt deeply sad and got lost in her feelings of pain and loss. Anita's real problem was that she did not know how to handle her hurt feelings, and the pain they caused her stopped her from properly practicing the HEAL method. Her feelings were so strong that she did not practice my HEAL method but rather her own painful version of it.

Anita started her practice with good intentions. Her H statement was "I hoped my marriage to John would be mutually satisfying and last until we died." This was a fine H statement. It was personal, specific, and positive. She acknowledged that she had hoped for a sound marriage instead of having created an unenforceable rule about *having* to have a sound marriage. However, Anita had problems with her E statement. Instead of reminding herself that "I understand and accept that some relationships fail, even with the best intentions of the partners," she phrased her statement as an unenforceable rule: "I know that some relationships may end, but it is not okay that mine failed. My husband was wrong to mess things up the way he did."

Anita's pain was normal in the face of sadness and loss. Her relationship had ended badly and caused her a lot of anguish. It was important that Anita realize she would eventually learn to bear her sadness. At some point her sadness, like any other emotion, would pass. I asked her whether, even now, she was always sad. No, she said, admitting that when she snuggled with her children she even felt good. I asked her whether she always felt good, and again she said no. I asked her whether she ever felt happy and sad in the same day. Yes, she said. I asked her to remember something sad from her past. Then I asked her to remember something happy from her past. Did each of these feelings change and go away? Anita replied that, yes, they did. With this exercise, I was able to gently remind her that even her current feelings would change and go away someday.

I explained to Anita that it is possible to gain control of our emotions eventually because they are constantly changing. If one feeling remained constant, there would be no way to change it. Our feelings are directly related to how we think and what we pay attention to, so it is useful to know how to change what we think and notice. I suggested that Anita practice the HEAL method even when she felt sad and that she pay more attention to the practice than to how she felt at each moment. In some ways practicing the HEAL method is like taking medicine: you need to take your medicine even when you do not feel like it, because that is the only way you can know if the medicine works.

I offered Anita one strong caveat to my advice: if her sad feelings proved overwhelming, interfered with her normal activities, such as eating and sleeping, kept her isolated, or caused her to feel suicidal, she should speak with a trained counselor. At that point, trying to forgive her husband would not be her first concern. I make that same suggestion to anyone reading this book. If you are suffering from disturbing physical symptoms or disabling emotional pain, please find an appropriate therapist or medical doctor for a consultation.

Here is another important caveat: don't try to practice HEAL when your hurts are still very new. Anita came to see me several months after her separation. If she had come to see me any sooner, I would have suggested that she be patient with herself. When the pain is still very fresh, the best thing you can do is treat yourself with kindness and experience the hurt and sadness that come with loss. I work with many people who are more comfortable with their painful feelings than they are with the idea of trying to feel better. These people struggle to trust their warm and loving feelings. Their painful feelings are like annoying relatives who come for a visit and then do not leave.

Unfortunately, being stuck in pain causes many people to forget that negative feelings are no more real and lasting than positive feelings. The continued practice of PERT and HEAL can be very helpful for people in this situation.

A Is for Affirm

Before we go on to the next component of the HEAL method, remember that you begin the practice with a brief period of soft belly breathing. Then you think of someone you love or something wonderful and keep your attention on the area around your heart. At the same time, you continue to breathe slowly and deeply into and out of your belly. Then you craft appropriate H and E statements. The next step in the HEAL method is to "Affirm" your positive intention.

Positive intention is the motivation you had for staying in the painful situation in the first place. Your motivation is always to create something positive in your relationship and not just hope that bad things don't happen. Your positive intention is defining what you wanted and expressing it in the most positive terms you can find.

Jessica wanted a loving relationship with her husband Ralph. Her positive intention was to create a loving partnership that would thrive on good communication and loving intimacy. A positive intention refers both to the specific relationship and to the bigger, long-term picture. Jessica's positive intention was a loving marriage, and she tried her utmost to make that happen with Ralph. However, her larger goal was not limited to her marriage to Ralph. Jessica understood that she would have the same positive intention no matter who her partner might be in the future.

Jessica's big-picture goal was to learn how to create a good relationship, preferably with Ralph. She might have to enter counseling, confront her husband, read books on relationships, or talk to successfully coupled people in order to learn how to do this. She might have to ask friends and lovers to give her honest feedback. There were many ways to improve her marriage to Ralph, but if it still ended, she could use what she learned to make her next relationship better. Jessica's positive intention put her positive goal in the center and her relationship problems at the periphery. The key for Jessica was to not allow her problems with Ralph to sidetrack her from her goal of a good relationship.

To find your positive intention, ask the following question: *how would my life be better if I was able to improve the situation that is causing me pain?* You could also ask yourself: *what is my reason for being in this situation in the first place?*

Seth had had a difficult relationship with his in-laws from the very start. His mother-in-law was always cold and critical with him, yet greeted the rest of his family with warmth and affection. When Seth fell very ill, his mother-in-law was indifferent to his suffering. She made it clear that she looked down on him for being messy, since she maintained high standards of cleanliness in her home. Seth and his wife fought every time they visited her parents, and by the time he came to my class he was sick of the situation.

When Seth sat down to write his positive intention, he was astounded to realize that he had no positive interest in his mother-in-law. He would have liked it if she mellowed out and treated him better, but the truth was that she was unimportant to him. The only reason he visited her was to support his wife and help her to stay in touch with her family. Seth suddenly realized that if his behavior was hurting his wife, then he was not living his positive intention. Realizing this, he changed his positive intention: to lovingly support his wife by remaining unruffled by his mother-in-law.

Our positive intention can also remind us that any hurtful experience can help us grow and give us a reason to move forward. Our positive intention might be the desire to learn from our relationship problems and become a better partner. We can use what we have learned to become stronger and more compassionate lovers. By acknowledging what didn't work in our relationship, we can vow to never do those things again. To *affirm* your positive intention reconnects you with a reason to move forward and turns your attention from what is not working to what it is you want to go well. You go from lamenting what failed or hurt to acknowledging your ability to find a good reason to continue.

I like to use the following image to help people understand what I mean by positive intention. Imagine that positive intentions are winding roads that take you from one part of your life to another. Many of us have positive intentions for our relationships such as creating a loving family, developing a long-term and loving partnership, creating economic security for the family, having a truly intimate connection, developing good communication, having a mutually satisfying sex life, creating beauty together, and nurturing personal growth. Imagine that your positive intention is a road and that you are driving on that road toward your goals.

Perhaps you are forty-seven and struggling to keep the passion alive with your husband. Your goal of having a loving marriage with a good sex life may be taking a hit; you've had a tire blowout on the relationship road. You are confused and scared because you've never had to change a tire before. Perhaps you know how, but you let your spare tire get flat, and you are struggling to use an underinflated tire. Maybe your son took the spare tire out of the trunk and never put it back in. As you struggle to figure out your problem, you wonder when the next highway patrol officer will come by. Throughout this experience, you are probably muttering under your breath that you do not have time for this and are late for an important meeting.

This metaphorical flat tire is standing in for things that can derail us on the road to intimacy. Often we do not know how to fix the hole in our heart. Many of us will not have prepared ourselves for the struggle that a successful relationship entails. Many people let their friendship with their spouse wither, and too often partners take each other for granted. Some people will deal with the crisis by crafting a story about how terrible it was to be stuck. They will stay stuck on the side of the road complaining about how unfair life is.

Now, shift your thinking to understand that life often forces us to modify our plans and that it is normal to get flat tires. Tell yourself that you can choose how long it takes you to get back on the road. You can choose to stay on the side of the road for years, afraid to get back behind the wheel, or you can fix your flat and move on. You may well get another flat tire one day; dangers always lurk, and we are never certain of safety. Remember that life goes on, and it is up to you to fix your problem and keep going.

Now picture yourself fixing the tire, patting yourself on the back for taking care of yourself, and simply starting out again. By doing this, you are connecting to your positive intention. Your positive intention is the motivation that enables you to fix your tire, make peace with the disruption, and move forward again as best you can. The good news is that as we connect to our positive intention, we begin to find forgiveness. Forgiveness is the compassion we experience as we remind ourselves that by driving a car—having a relationship—we run the risk of a breakdown. Forgiveness is the power we get as we assert that we have a deep well of resilience to draw upon. Forgiveness is the grace that helps us remember to look around while we're on the side of the road and appreciate our beautiful surroundings and the people we love. To help forgiveness emerge, we can learn to see ourselves from the point of view of our positive intention, not primarily as a wounded or rejected lover.

L Is for Long-Term

The L in HEAL stands for making a Long-term commitment to your long-range well-being by committing to the discipline to follow your positive intention and to practice the HEAL method whenever you feel upset over a past hurt. This component of the method emphasizes the importance of practice. When you commit to a long-term practice, you are committing to telling your story from your new point of view based in your positive intention. This commitment strengthens you whenever you feel the temptation to go back to your old way of seeing your situation—say, as a wounded lover. Crafting your L statement is the final part of the HEAL method.

A strong L statement commits you to practice the HEAL method and follow your positive intention. Every L statement includes the following: "I make the *long-term commitment* to follow my positive intention and use the HEAL method." For many of you, this statement will be sufficient.

However, some people find that they can't manifest their positive intention without learning new skills. Their L statement thus would add: "I make a *long-term commitment* to learn the specific new skills I need to prosper." My patients have developed these skills through supportive services such as assertiveness training, stress management, sex therapy, communication skills, twelve-step programs, and individual or couple counseling. In addition, there are a few more simple techniques that almost anyone would find helpful.

The first technique is to look for people who have successfully healed from a wound similar to the one that troubles you. Since almost all of our relationship problems arise from common experiences, you should be able to find those who have mastered your own particular difficulty. Through sharing your experiences and listening to theirs, you can learn how to overcome your pain and move on with your life. Listen to what other people say, and determine how you can incorporate their lessons into your life. Try to model your behavior after the successful behavior of others. Terry took this advice to heart.

Terry struggled with his wife's seeming indifference to their economic well-being. He realized that he had to change how he looked at his problem with his wife. When he made an effort to find people who'd experienced a similar situation with a financially incompatible spouse, he was fortunate to meet another man who had dealt with a very similar problem in his marriage. Terry felt heard and supported by his new friend and was reminded that he had some difficult choices to make. What this friend offered Terry was a successful model of good coping, help in asserting himself, and the knowledge that even in difficult situations he still had choices.

The second technique is to ask a friend or family member to let you know when you are complaining too much. A good friend of Terry's took on the responsibility of stopping him whenever he complained about his wife's terrible spending habits and indifference to saving money. Choose someone you trust and ask that person to gently remind you when you slip back into bad habits. The friend does not need to do anything more than point out when you are about to start complaining. You can then choose to refocus on your positive intention.

A third simple technique is to give yourself permission to mull over the grievance for a short period each day. Diana felt that one reason she had been cheated out of a promotion was that her husband would not take any responsibility for child care. She still had some issues about this but decided that she would dwell on them only at 7:00 P.M. each evening. She gave herself fifteen minutes a day to think about how she had been wronged. Every night Diana sat down at the kitchen table at seven and asked herself whether she needed to vent. Many times she did not, but if she did, she wrote her feelings down and then got up and had dinner. She also practiced PERT or looked for something to watch on her gratitude or beauty channels. By doing this, Diana was able to keep the rest of her day free from bitterness and anger. By writing down her feelings, she was also able to keep track of how she was coping with the perceived injustice.

The final technique is to reward yourself for practicing the techniques offered in this book. Terry kept a journal and noted down every time he practiced the HEAL method. When he practiced more than five times a day, he treated himself with a great dessert. If he'd practiced more than forty times by the end of the week, he rewarded himself with a massage.

Ruth decided that she and her husband would have to get counseling if their marriage was going to work. Her first L statement was a simple promise to practice HEAL and remain focused on her positive intention. However, Ruth's positive intention was personal growth. She quickly realized that she lacked any real personal growth skills because she had spent so many years locked in bitterness. In addition to counseling, Ruth committed herself to practicing PERT on a daily basis and taking a meditation class. The next time we spoke she came up with a new L statement that committed her to experiment with and learn a variety of personal growth skills.

When Sandra joined my class, I gave her the goal of practicing the HEAL method every day for two weeks. For the first three days I told her to do the full HEAL practice twice a day. This took her about twenty-five minutes a day to do. As she practiced, Sandra found that she could repeat the HEAL statements to herself more quickly. After ten brief practice attempts, she could be done in ten minutes. Sandra took the bait: after a couple of days she noticed that her sad story was beginning to change. The results were fleeting at first, but by the end of the first week she started to see changes in her mood and temperament. By the end of two weeks of practice she was convinced that her present relationship with her husband, even after the stroke, was more important than what she had lost. Sandra finally accepted that she could never recover the past. She saw also that it was love that kept her in her marriage. She could accept errors she had made that were grounded in love. Love was her positive intention.

Sandra now realized that she had been afraid of confrontation her whole life and had always been a little scared to demand anything from her husband. She realized that this was a pattern in all of her relationships. As a result, she decided to take an assertiveness class to learn how to get what she wanted. Sandra knew the assertiveness training would help her grow as a person, whether or not it helped her marriage. After three weeks of grieving the years wasted and affection denied, she finally forgave her husband. She was able to let go of the resentment she felt for the way he had neglected her in favor of his work. She was now able to accept his humanness and to understand that the hurt she felt was fleeting. Understanding that they each had done the best they could, she found peace. As she forgave her husband, Sandy noticed an awakening in her heart and a renewed tenderness toward him, diminished capacity and all.

HEAL Method Guided Practice (Full Version)

1. Think of a wound or loss in your relationship that you could imagine feeling differently about.

2. Practice PERT for two or three minutes.

3. Focus your attention in the area around your heart. Ensure that you are breathing slowly and deeply into and out of your belly.

4. Reflect for a moment on what you would have preferred to have seen happen in this specific situation. Make an H statement to reflect a *hope* that is personal, specific, and positive.

5. Hold your H statement in your heart.

6. When the H statement is clear, *educate* yourself about the limitations in demanding that things always work out the way you want.

7. Make your E statement broad, and in your heart understand and accept that you are okay even though not all your hopes can be realized.

8. *Affirm* your positive intention with an A statement—the positive long-term goal underneath the hope you had for this specific situation.

9. With determination, hold your A statement in the warm feelings in your heart. Repeat your positive intention a couple of times.

10. Make an L statement that stands for a *long-term commitment* to:

    Practice the HEAL method—both the full and brief versions

    Follow your positive intention, even when difficult

    Learn the skills you need to manifest your positive intention

11. Continue to breathe slowly and deeply into and out of your belly for another thirty seconds to a minute.

HEAL Method Guided Practice (Brief Version)

Anytime you feel hurt or anger over an unresolved grievance:

1. Bring your attention fully to your stomach as you slowly draw two slow, deep breaths in and out.

2. On the third inhalation, bring to your mind's eye an image of someone you love or of a beautiful scene in nature that fills you with awe and peace. You may have a stronger response if you imagine these positive feelings as centered in the area around your heart.

3. Continue to breathe slowly into and out of your belly.

4. Reflect on what you would have preferred to have seen happen in this specific situation.

5. Make a *hope* statement that is personal, specific, and positive.

6. Then *educate* yourself about the limitations in demanding that things always work out the way you want.

7. *Affirm* your positive intention—the positive, long-term goal underneath the hope you had for this specific grievance.

8. Make a *long-term commitment* to practice the HEAL method and follow your positive intention.

Practice the full version of the HEAL method at least once each day to get the full benefit. When you first begin, it is useful to practice twice each day. Try to practice the full HEAL method every day for at least a week. After a couple of days, you will be familiar enough with the method to try the brief version. By practicing HEAL, you can grieve your loss and allow yourself to recover the loving, positive direction that was behind many of your actions. You might find it helpful to repeat the following silently: *hope, educate, affirm, long-term.* Allow these words to circulate in the area around your heart, and remember that through them you are working hard to grieve your wounds and to make peace and forgiveness your reality.

◆

TEN

Step 6:
Choose to Recommit

A good relationship is worth the effort of letting go of an annoying trait in your partner and being as kind as possible to this person you are connected to. Those two ideas are central to your marriage vows. A marriage is a choice to recommit to your partner every day. Every spouse, whether recovering from a brutal betrayal or simply dealing with a sloppy partner, decides every day whether to get up and dance with that partner again. Every marriage goes through periods when each partner is not sure about continuing it. This chapter is about this idea that forgiveness is based upon a continual recommitment to your relationship. Forgiveness comes after grieving your losses, and it allows you to move forward in your relationship with happiness and a positive attitude. This is true whether the losses were big (your spouse is a drug addict) or little (your lazy partner never does the grocery run) or somewhere in between—as when you accept the fact that you married a slob, you have grieved the neat person you should have married, and you have recommitted to the lovable human being you chose to be with.

Recommitting is an ongoing process; you have to recommit every time your lover says the same dumb thing again and you react with your same exasperated sigh. You have to recommit when your lover is late yet again, or leaves a cheap tip for the third time in a week. If your partner does something annoying but ultimately insignificant, acknowledge your dismay or loss for an instant and then connect right back again. Try saying something to help put the annoyance in perspective and get back in the game. You could remind yourself that "she's worth it," or "it was no big deal." Most of the time you don't even need to let your lover know he or she has done anything wrong.

It is always up to you to decide whether to tell your partner you are upset with his or her behavior. If your partner has done something really bad, the grief process described in the last chapter will help. In this chapter, you will learn that telling the right story about your relationship can lead to kinder speech and allow you truly to recommit to your loved one. The way we talk about our marriage is critical; our words can help make an experience either "good" or "bad." Think about how you react to something bad in your relationship; your response is probably almost instant as your stomach tightens and your thoughts turn negative. This type of response often happens so fast that we barely know why. Learning how to quickly reconnect rather than allow feelings to remain negative is critical.

The good news is that the story you tell about your relationship has more to do with creating your shared future than the specific things that happen to you. If you tell a cold and unloving story, it can damage your relationship, whereas a loving and forgiving story can help strengthen the love you feel for your partner. The health of your relationship is largely up to you. Most couples have difficult experiences over the course of their marriage, and many get through them more or less intact. The type of story the couple tells about these experiences can have a great impact on how their relationship turns out.

A hopeful and loving story enriches and positively defines your relationship, while a pessimistic and blame-filled story is poison. If you talk with scorn and self-pity about how awful it is to deal with your lover's ugly habits, you are going to hurt your relationship. A healing and positive spin on your experience, on the other hand, will help make your partner feel loved and wanted. This chapter contrasts grievance stories with stories of forgiveness and describes a couple of excellent strategies for talking about your partner that facilitate healing and forgiveness.

Whenever possible, you want to speak of your lover and your relationship with kindness. That is the overarching message of this book. Look for any way you can to be kind to the person you share your life with. Don't be tempted to say nasty things when your lover screws up or to put your lover down when he or she fails. While such negative responses are normal and occasionally useful, in the long run they hurt your partner's feelings. Telling our partners that we do not like their unkind words is one thing—in fact, this can be helpful to defend ourselves and provide good boundaries if we feel insulted—but it is less useful to tell friends how insensitive our lovers are or to accuse them of insensitivity over and over. Setting boundaries and expressing ourselves is good, but talking about our relationship negatively and highlighting our lover's failings is bad.

So the first lesson is to be careful about choosing the times when you say things to your lover that are not kind. Instead of being critical, try to talk about your partner's good points as often as possible. You have more control over the words you speak than anything else in life, and every moment you can make the choice between using positive language or negative language. The best contribution you can make to your marriage is the quality of the words you use.

Picture yourself driving along on the freeway and being cut off by a speeding driver. Your car isn't damaged, but you have to brake quickly to get out of the way. Most drivers in this situation will curse the other driver for a moment. Other normal responses that do not include harsh words or actions might be deep breathing or feeling lucky that nothing bad happened. However, the most important thing is to feel your negative reaction and then let it go when the erratic driver has passed. Unfortunately, too many of us continue to curse the bad driver long afterward. Some people intensify the stress of the situation by making a cell phone call to tell a family member or friend about the awful people on the road.

Being cut off caused you to be verbally protective of yourself and to curse the bad driver—a normal reaction to the situation. After that protective response, you can choose what to do next. Either you can choose to continue being harsh and angry, or you can find another approach. This choice will be influenced by your past habits and your mood at the time. The same is true in your relationship, the health of which depends on the choices you make in how you talk to your partner. Remember that what comes out of your mouth says more about your character than it does about your partner's. If Sarah screams at her husband Jose, she is saying more about herself than she is about him. Every time we talk we are giving those around us a snapshot of our character, both our strengths and our weaknesses. We think that we are describing our lover's weaknesses, but our words and actions are actually showing our own.

This is true of people I work with every day. My patient Susan would get furious when she talked about her ex-husband. At the end of our conversations, I still knew very little about her ex but understood a whole lot about her problem with anger and blame. Susan thought that she could hide her character flaws by talking about those of her husband. The bottom line is that when we talk harshly, we are showing what pisses us off. When we are unforgiving, we show our true relationship to forgiveness. This does not excuse our lover's flaws, but just as our lovers reveal their character through their actions, so do we reveal our own character in how we speak and behave. In your primary relationship, you want to show your good qualities as much as you can.

The truth is that we can choose how we talk to and about our partner. Sadly, many people choose to discuss their lover negatively. When Sally moaned about Bill to her mother, she saw that as a normal thing to do, not an aggressive act against Bill. When Bill complained to his coworkers that Sally wouldn't let him watch the big game on TV, he thought it was her fault that he sounded as angry as he did. Kelly thought that by telling her husband she was ticked off by his attitude she was responding to his actions, not revealing her own weak conflict resolution skills. A lot of relationships struggle with the cost of holding a grudge and the sense of blame it causes. Getting rid of the blame quickly and regularly is hugely important if you want your relationship to thrive and move forward.

So, when dealing with minor offenses in your marriage, there are only a few instances in which harsh speech is even useful. In most small situations, you should be ready to move forward and recommit to your relationship after simply grieving the annoyance. Moving forward "without prejudice" is another way of saying "with forgiveness." You will go a long way toward doing this simply by speaking about and to your partner with kindness rather than cruelty. When your partner has committed a bigger offense, you will have to grieve your loss. You do not have to suffer alone: you will probably need to share your sense of pain and violation. Remember, however, that to move forward you need to have empowering stories to tell about your marriage.

In the last chapter, I talked about how positive intention can help you in your relationship. Positive intention is shorthand for talking about why you want your relationship to succeed, or what you are going to do to make it work, or how you can grow from a challenging experience. It is the opposite of complaining. Positive intention helps you see the big picture of a successful relationship and stops you from focusing on the little picture of disappointment or grievance. In this chapter, I want to reiterate the need for a positive take on your marriage as well as broaden the concept of positive intention. I want you to share stories with yourself, with your loved one, and with your friends and family that reflect a strong and positive commitment to your marriage. These stories do not have to be long or detailed, but they should anchor your relationship in the idea of goodness and the continued possibility of success.

To find your positive intention, try rephrasing the following questions as they might relate to your situation: *How would my life be better if the problem with my lover had worked out differently? How would I benefit if my husband obeyed my request and was neater in the house? Would our marriage be stronger if my wife had not had an affair?*

Ask yourself: *what is my reason for being in this situation in the first place?* That reason will help you frame your goals for your relationship in strictly positive terms.

Finding Your Positive Intention

1. Find a quiet place where you can be undisturbed for about five minutes.

2. Practice PERT once or twice to get yourself into a relaxed and open-hearted frame of mind.

3. Ask the loving part of yourself: *what is my reason for having the particular grievance I have right now?*

4. Write down your response in positive terms only, then edit until you have a one- or two-sentence positive intention.

5. Promise yourself that you will not tell the grievance story any longer.

6. Practice telling the positive intention story to yourself a couple of times before you share it with anyone else.

Positive intentions allow you to keep the good reasons for staying in your marriage at the front of your thoughts. Those good reasons revolve around why you are there and what hope the relationship holds for you. One good reason could be something you want to accomplish together, such as create a strong family or work hard to afford a house. Your positive intention might be about how you want to treat your lover, perhaps by being kinder or more respectful. Maybe you want to help your lover heal from pain he or she experienced in childhood. Perhaps you want to repay your lover for all the goodwill shown to you. Your positive intention is the positive motivation you bring to the marriage. Remember to access it and talk about it on a regular basis.

You do not have to create one all-purpose positive intention. It is good to have both content and process goals. Content goals are the tangible things that you want to do in your marriage, such as create a family or work to buy a home. These goals could be about your children, your retirement plans, or a desire for great sex. Process goals are your positive intentions about how you are going to get to where you want to go in your marriage. A process goal could be about patience or a strong desire to communicate. Or it could be a commitment to stop being angry with your lover or simply to do your best to be a loving partner. When you can reflect on and talk about the many positive goals you have for your relationship, your bond with your partner will grow stronger.

When you have been hurt or annoyed by your partner's behavior, you will need to connect with your positive intention story in order to move forward. For example, Sarah's positive intention was to create a safe and loving home for her children. She realized that her bitterness and resentment toward Howard was moving her further away from her positive goals. Disappointment is inevitable in a relationship, but harping on it is a choice. Sarah realized that it was more important to talk about her loving goals for her marriage. Ingrid was irritated by her husband's excessive sexual demands, but she learned to keep connected to her intention to successfully negotiate their sexual differences. Ingrid understood that it was more important to the health of her relationship to negotiate their differences than to criticize Jake. Treating Jake like the enemy would only hurt their relationship. He was just a person she loved who had different ways of behaving sexually than she did.

Ultimately we all need to understand and practice the lesson that Ingrid learned. Turning our differences and our different realities into adversarial situations is a mistake. What we need to do is practice forgiveness and find a good way to talk about the challenges of a marriage. When you speak positively, you are better able to articulate the loving reasons you are in the relationship and you and your partner are more likely to grow together and thrive. Your marriage gives you untold opportunities to practice kinder speech and more forgiving attitudes. Your lover will be gracious enough to challenge your assumptions and courageous enough to be different from you. You can trust me on this. Practicing this sixth step by offering kind words and positive intention stories will be helpful to both of you.

The sixth step is an easy-to-follow, proven road map to forgiveness. You now have the tools you need to be forgiving of your partner. You have six simple strategies that will make you a more giving and open-hearted lover. You will be a much nicer person to be around, and you will give your partner ample opportunity to feel cared for and appreciated.

Once again, these are the steps you need to follow to have a successful marriage: honor your choice of partner, accept that your partner is flawed, look for the good in your partner, give your lover a break, grieve your losses, and offer kind words. All that's left to learn is how to be gentle and forgiving with yourself as well as with your partner. In the last chapter, I will give you some tips on how to do that.

———◆———

ELEVEN

Step 7:
Please Give Yourself a Break

Modern life is hectic, and both you and your partner are likely to be busy, self-absorbed, and idiosyncratic individuals. Because of this, you often have to give your lover a break if you want to make your relationship work and sustain the connection. The reality that you are as stressed, quirky, and self-interested as your partner makes your relationship even more demanding. Just like your loved one, you can fail at aspects of your relationship and do things without thinking or examining the consequences. This difficult truth does not disqualify either of you from being loved or from doing your best. It just means that a lot of forgiveness is needed on both sides and toward each other. The final lesson of this book is that you can and should apply to yourself the practices and insights I have shared here. So many couples spend their lives trapped in guilt and shame over their past actions. People feel paralyzed because they have never forgiven themselves for failures of one kind or another. It is often harder to forgive yourself than it is to forgive others.

It is important to be gentle with and accepting of yourself throughout your relationship. You are just as flawed, misguided, and hurtful as your lover, and you both need a good dose of

TLC. While the idea of self-forgiveness might be a "duh" to many of you, the point still needs to be made. Self-forgiveness enables you to move on with kindness after grieving your flaws and the ways you have hurt your lover. When you forgive yourself, you look for your good qualities, appreciate the love you offer, and accept with humility the harm you cause. You also change your story to reflect your positive intention and your effort to do the best you can with what you have to work with.

Self-forgiveness is not that different from forgiving your partner. My program teaches that forgiving one kind of offense is much the same as forgiving another. In most ways, self-forgiveness follows the same process as interpersonal forgiveness. The overriding goal of forgiveness, to experience peace in your life, is the same. We need to be able to accept our mistakes and correct them as necessary. We do not need to suffer needlessly. We can forgive ourselves for failing, make the necessary amends and changes, and move on to honor our positive intention.

There are four categories of self-forgiveness. Remember that not all day-to-day instances of self-forgiveness are as dramatic as my examples. The first category covers people who are upset with themselves for not accomplishing one of the important tasks of a successful relationship, such as getting married at what they feel would have been the "right" age, having children, or making a good living. People who do not meet their personal relationship goals feel that they have been a failure and constantly criticize themselves for it. The second category covers people who failed to take action at a point in their lives when it seemed important. Perhaps they failed to help a loved one in a timely fashion. The third category covers people who hurt someone and are angry at themselves for it. People who cheated on a lover or spouse, behaved terribly as a parent, or did poorly in business fall into this category. The fourth category covers people whose lives have been filled with self-destructive behavior, such as alcohol abuse or an unwillingness to work hard.

Toni was a woman in her late forties. She was unable to forgive herself for allowing her family to get into debt. Toni felt that she had failed at an important life task, and she literally loathed herself for the economic choices she had made. Toni worked for many years as a preschool teacher. She loved her job, appreciated the small children she worked with, and felt that she was contributing to the world through her work. Even though her husband Marvin often pointed out that her low-paying career choice was putting a financial strain on them, Toni was unwilling to give up a career she liked so much.

Toni and Marvin were married for fifteen years and had two children when he died after a lengthy illness. Suddenly Toni's family was in serious financial difficulty. Toni had never imagined that she might have to raise her kids on her own, but it soon became clear that her job didn't pay enough to support them. Toni felt tremendously angry with herself for not adequately anticipating her future financial needs.

Larry falls into the second category. His wife Noreen and his father had a terrible relationship for years, and Larry hated that he hadn't supported or protected her. During the nine years they had been married, Larry's father had insulted Noreen every time he saw her and regularly told Larry that he'd married the wrong woman. Larry, for reasons that were related to his upbringing, allowed his father to do this. Noreen fought back against her father-in-law and regularly told Larry how much she was hurt by his father's behavior. Even Larry was sick of his father's insults. He did not like the way Noreen acted, but he knew that it was a response to his father's cruelty and she would stop if he did. Larry was bitterly disappointed in his inability to confront and stop his father. Larry said he could forgive his father for being such an asshole, but could not forgive himself for not protecting his wife.

Doreen, who struggled to forgive herself for having hurt someone else, falls into the third category of self-forgiveness offenses. Doreen ended her fifteen-year marriage to John by having an affair with a business associate. She realized that her marriage had been troubled for years before she cheated. She and her husband had barely had sex for the last two years of their marriage, and the sex was lethargic and sporadic even before then. Doreen and John often went weeks without sleeping together. John was quite successful, made a lot of money, and traveled all over the world. He barely noticed their troubles because he loved his work and spent so many nights away from home. Doreen struggled to deal with getting older and the imminent departure of their two teenage children.

Doreen was so undone by her husband's neglect and by impending middle age that she initiated an affair with a business associate who had lost his wife to cancer. The affair lasted only six months, but it was so passionate and exciting that she knew her marriage was over. Doreen ended the affair and her marriage at the same time. Her husband moved out of the house, and her children spent every other weekend with him.

Doreen dated some, but when she started feeling guilty about what her affair had done to her husband and children she stopped. She really regretted that she and her husband had not gone into counseling. There were other causes of the marital breakup, but Doreen's guilt over the affair was paralyzing.

Elaine was a newly married woman who at the age of thirty-three decided she had to clean up her life. Her mother had died when she was thirty-two, and Elaine did not want her own life to follow that sad pattern. Elaine found changing her behavior and forgiving herself to be more difficult tasks than she had anticipated. Her mom had married a couple of times and rarely had either a steady job or a steady relationship. Her mother had loved Elaine and always treated her with as much kindness as she could. She had also had a drinking problem, however, and struggled to gain the skills necessary for long-term employment.

When Elaine was fifteen, she started using marijuana. Then she started drinking every weekend and had numerous brief affairs, even after getting married. Her marriage was stormy, but she loved her husband. Her husband wanted kids, but Elaine was afraid that she would be as bad a mother as hers had been. When she hit thirty-three, Elaine realized that she needed to learn some new habits or she would end up like her mother. Elaine found it incredibly hard to forgive herself, however, for her history of self-destructive behavior.

Toni was depressed about the loss of her husband, her low-paying job, and her sense of being a failure. She made her difficult situation much worse by condemning herself for it. She thought that she should have been able to get a better job and do right by her kids.

Larry was a successful businessman with a great marriage, but he still thought of himself as a failure because he did not stand up to his father. Larry lived every day like he was still failing to stand up to his dad. If someone praised Larry, he thought they were joking. If people only knew the real, wimpy Larry, he thought, they would never praise him.

Doreen's story was dominated by regrets and anger over her affair. She condemned herself for ending a marriage that had been broken for years. She saw herself as a bad person rather than as a woman who had made a poor decision under stress.

Elaine was making a positive decision by trying to change the direction of her life, but the way she thought about it was wrong. She needed to realize that the past was done and that all she could control was her future.

All these people needed to practice self-forgiveness and move forward in their lives. Using forgiveness tools would work for them because all grievances emerge from a negative response to not getting what you want. You can use PERT to successfully change your feelings, whether you are forgiving yourself or another person. The same "unenforceable rules" that can cause you to create a grievance in your relationship with another can also cause you to create a grievance with yourself. The HEAL method will work whether you are forgiving yourself or forgiving others. Likewise, you can use your remote to change the channel on your personal TV when you are feeling angry and unforgiving toward yourself. It is as important to look for the good in yourself as it is to find the good in your partner. And sometimes you have to feel the grief over the harm you have done or the things you failed to do before you can move on.

The good news about self-forgiveness is that, because we have more power over our own actions than we do over the actions of our partners, it can be easier than forgiving your lover. Interpersonal forgiveness is difficult precisely because we cannot change the way our partners act. The vulnerability caused by our limited control is at the heart of many of the "unenforceable rules" we create. We want our lovers to treat us a certain way, and unfortunately they often choose to treat us the way they want to. Darlene wanted her spouse to stop cheating on her and recommit to a loving relationship. Mary wanted her partner to help with the children instead of spending his weekends golfing. Lorraine wanted her husband to succeed at work, but he had been unemployed for months. None of these women was able to control the actions of the most important person in her life.

We have more control over our own actions than over the actions of our partner. We can always learn new ways to do old things, and we have the freedom to experiment with acting in different ways until we find a way that works. We can talk to people who are successful and find out how they do what they do. We can change our behavior in many different ways, but we have very limited power to change the behavior of others, even our lover. True self-forgiveness happens only when we accept that we don't have control over anyone, even ourselves.

Nobody is perfect, and everybody will make many mistakes. Some of us make mistakes that cause harm, and others make mistakes that only cause a mess. Because you and your partner are human beings, you will make mistakes, fail occasionally, and sometimes even harm other people. Your need to be perfect is an unenforceable rule, one that can never be met. Needing to never hurt your lover is an unenforceable rule. Demanding that you always be successful in all aspects of your relationship is an unenforceable rule. When you accept that you are human, you are able to offer forgiveness to yourself and remember that you have the resources at your disposal to improve yourself and help others.

Our habits are the biggest block between ourselves and self-forgiveness and new ways of behaving. We all have habits that are difficult to change. Remember Larry? Whenever his dad insulted either him or his wife, Larry shut down inside. He felt afraid to say anything to his father and then hated himself for letting his dad get away with being abusive to his wife. Larry's self-forgiveness hinged on his ability to become more assertive and at the same time forgive the ways in which he had not adequately asserted himself in the past.

There are two ways in which it would have been easier for Larry to forgive himself than forgive his dad. First, Larry had the ability to change his own behavior, but he could not force his father to change. Larry could make the choice to act differently, but he couldn't choose how his dad behaved.

Even though Larry had never fought back with words, he changed his behavior by learning to communicate more effectively with his father. After many years of frustration and lots of false starts, Larry finally learned how to speak assertively and demand respect. Larry's father had brutalized him as a kid, but at thirty-five Larry finally learned to stand up to him. Part of Larry's forgiveness journey was to learn to tell his dad each time his boundary was crossed by his dad's behavior.

Doreen chose to deal with her situation by learning new behaviors. She entered counseling to help get over her marriage and figure out why she had stayed in it so long. Doreen also decided that if her next partner traveled a lot, she would go with him when she could.

The second advantage to self-forgiveness is that you can make amends for your actions. Once you have forgiven yourself, you can try to heal the harm you have done and improve situations where you have created harm or loss. When you need to forgive someone else, you cannot guarantee that that person will apologize or do anything to make the situation better. After the affair, Doreen apologized to her husband on a number of occasions and made it a point to support the way he parented their children. Larry apologized to Noreen and learned to take her side when she complained about his father.

To make amends you look for a way to be kind to those you have hurt. Elaine joined a twelve-step program and embraced the steps about making amends. She worked hard at communicating with her husband about her problem and offered to enter counseling to work out the issue of having children. When the people you have hurt are dead or otherwise unavailable, you can provide a symbolic kindness to someone else. If you were cruel in a past relationship, you can be more loving in a current one. If you failed your children when they were young, you can make amends by tutoring special needs students. If you stole money years ago, you can donate to charity now to try to symbolically mend the situation. At a minimum, you can begin by offering a sincere apology for bad behavior. If the person you hurt was yourself, you can try talking about yourself with kindness. Highlight your good points and articulate your strengths. Reward your positive changes and forgive the ways in which you have failed.

Larry and Doreen showed me that a long-standing grievance against yourself can hurt as much as or more than a grievance held against someone else. All grievances begin when we don't get the outcome we had hoped for. Once this happens, we throw in an "unenforceable rule" such as "I should have known better" or "I always need to do the right thing," and we begin to feel helpless, angry, and upset. Slowly, we start to be burdened by shame and guilt on top of the anger and guilt we already feel.

Like Larry, you may think you should have taken action long ago. Larry's continued anger at himself did not help him take constructive action. The truth is that Larry was not able to stop his father until he was ready. If you are like Elaine, you may hate the way you lived a part of your life. However, Elaine could not change her life until she had proper training and sufficient motivation. She needed the self-care that came through forgiveness lessons.

Or, like Doreen and Toni, you may feel badly about decisions you made. Doreen was a lonely woman stuck in an empty marriage with an absent husband. She did not know the best way to work things out or end the marriage. So she had an affair with a recent widower who had his own issues to deal with. I did not support her affair. Had Doreen asked me sooner, I would have suggested ways to get her husband into marital counseling. However, Doreen quickly ended the affair and apologized to her husband many times over. She did her best to make amends and understood clearly that she would never do this again.

Toni was guilty of nothing more than being a bad financial planner and not realizing that an untimely death could harm her family. Toni's poor-paying job, coupled with her husband's death, drastically changed her life circumstances. She now faced the demanding task of learning new job skills and letting go of a job she loved. At first Toni beat herself up for getting into this predicament and facing such a difficult transition. Toni needed to forgive herself. It is easier to forgive yourself if you realize that you are not alone in whatever you did wrong. Remember, every mistake you make has been made thousands of times by other people. You haven't created a new evil or a new way to fail. What you did was to react to a common human difficulty in a common way. The unkind things you have done are in the past. By using self-forgiveness, you can learn and practice better ways to act.

When you understand that you are human and will make mistakes, you will be able to take things less personally and feel encouraged to forgive yourself. Doing unkind things and occasionally failing is simply part of being human. But choosing to forgive ourselves, learn from our mistakes, and take the opportunity to grow is also part of being human. You can choose to continue to beat yourself up and stay stuck in anger at yourself, but shame, embarrassment, and guilt are emotions that do little to help us grow.

Everyone I've discussed in this chapter learned to practice PERT when they felt upset with themselves. Each of them now knows to create enforceable rules for themselves in the same way they would if their grievance were with their lover. My goal was to help Doreen, Larry, Toni, and Elaine take responsibility for how they felt. It pained me to see how their past actions paralyzed them in pain. I wanted to help them become more peaceful so that their grievance would rent less space in their minds. I didn't want Doreen, Larry, Toni, and Elaine to ignore their mistakes, and I wasn't trying to condone their actions. My goal was simply to teach them to forgive themselves so that they could learn and practice better ways of acting.

All four wanted to make changes in their lives. They saw that something needed to be done to improve the way they lived. Unfortunately, they had created more pain by harboring a grievance with themselves rather than grieving their losses and then making the necessary changes. Ultimately, they were able to forgive themselves because they changed their grievance stories to reflect their positive intention.

Toni, Elaine, Doreen, and Larry were taught to change their grievance story into a new story that reflected hope and positive intention. Toni's positive intention was to take good care of her children. She saw that this loving goal was behind her self-hatred and sense of failure. She was upset at herself for putting her children at risk. When Toni went back to school to learn computer technology, she reminded herself of the love she felt for her children, and that sustained her.

Elaine wanted to rescue herself from a difficult life. The death of her mother had triggered the loving part of herself into action. She changed her grievance story to reflect this kinder, more forgiving part of herself. Once Elaine was finally able to forgive herself, she could focus on her dreams and future goals rather than her painful past.

Doreen did not want to give up on marriage just because her first had ended badly. Her positive intention was to create a successful long-term relationship. In order to do this Doreen saw that she had to learn better communication skills to avoid the problems that occurred in her marriage to John. She realized that she needed to be more assertive and to not fool herself into thinking a flawed relationship would magically get better. After getting divorced and dating a little, Doreen decided that a new relationship would have to wait. She had been upset to realize that she was still capable of acting unkindly and doing things like having an affair. Therefore, she took it upon herself to develop new parts of herself with a therapist. She wanted to grow as a person in the hope of creating a stronger relationship with another man.

Larry's positive intention was to do what he could to support and honor his marriage. This meant that in any conflict he would side with Noreen, not his father. He would evaluate the success of his behavior in terms of how it helped his marriage, not how it affected him or his dad. When Larry was able to change how he approached the problem, Noreen became his ally and provided him with love and support. Larry realized that he was renting out too much mental space to his dad and that, as a result, there was insufficient room for Noreen. Larry's positive intention made his father's reactions less important to him and greatly increased Noreen's support of their marriage. They united and learned together how to talk assertively to Larry's father.

You can use HEAL to forgive yourself the same way you would use it to forgive your lover. The H in HEAL stands for hope. When you create an H statement, you are reminding yourself that you wished or hoped that you would behave in a certain way. You hoped to be a faithful spouse, to make good money, to get a specific job or promotion. You really wanted to be a caring parent, to keep the people you love safe, to treat your lover with respect and honesty. Larry wanted to maintain a loving relationship with Noreen even under the provocation of a difficult parent. He wanted to protect her from the insults of his father. His hope statement began with the word "I" and was focused on his specific goal. A useful H statement for Doreen might be: "I wanted to end my marriage to John by going to counseling and remaining faithful."

The E in HEAL stands for educate. Elaine still had moments of feeling despair or wanting drugs even as she made every attempt to reclaim her life, but that did not make her a failure—it made her human. She committed to change and was doing her best and awaiting the results. Elaine regularly reminded herself that taking two steps forward and one step backward was a fact of life.

Doreen's E statement might reflect the inherent limitations of human relationships. Her H and E statements could be something like: "I hoped to end my relationship with John in a kind manner, maintaining both his dignity and my own. I understand and accept that even with the best of intentions, many relationships end with human weakness and pain."

When making your E statement, remember that it has two parts. The first part is the general statement acknowledging that every hope carries with it the possibility of failure. For example, "I can only do my best," "Many good love affairs end in a messy way," and "Often parents have a hard time showing their love properly." For other people, a general statement might be "Partners are commonly disappointed in their lover's behavior" or "I may not be able to return my spouse's love exactly the way he/she wants." The second part of your E statement is about understanding and accepting the uncertainty of the first part.

I want to emphasize one point. Making an E statement does not mean that you condone your hurtful actions. What it does mean is that you regret what you did, but understand that it was also common behavior. You are disappointed by your actions, but determined to move forward and change your behavior. By making the statement, you are apologizing, hoping that you are forgiven, and working from this moment on to make amends for your actions. When you make an E statement, you are accepting that doing hurtful things and feeling pain are normal parts of being a human being.

The next step in the HEAL method, A, is to affirm your positive intention. Your positive intention might be about your goals and personal growth. If you are working on self-forgiveness, another useful positive intention is the desire to experience greater happiness. Try rewriting your story so that you can see your mistakes or poor choices as failed attempts to find happiness. Your positive intention goal now becomes to learn better ways to make yourself happy.

We all tend to beat ourselves up over the mistakes we have made. Elaine did this by dwelling on her failures and focusing on her drug misuse.

Elaine realized that her marijuana use and drinking was an attempt to make herself happy. She had an appropriate goal—happiness—but lacked the tools to get there yet. Elaine made her old idea that drugs could bring her happiness a part of her positive intention story. Her positive intention story went on to say that drugs proved to be a poor choice of tool for finding happiness. Elaine used her positive intention to tell herself that her happiness was important and that she was going to try more productive ways to make herself feel good.

The last step in HEAL, L, stands for making a long-term commitment to your well-being. Every L statement includes the following: "I make the long-term commitment to follow my positive intention and use the HEAL method." When you need to learn new skills in order to manifest your positive intention, you can add to your L statement: "I make a long-term commitment to learn whatever new skills I need to prosper."

When you are forgiving yourself, your L statement can also include your commitment to make amends to those you have hurt. Doreen used her L statement to remind herself that she wanted to treat John with kindness. Part of her positive intention was to encourage their children to visit John and to speak highly of him to their kids and friends. Larry reminded himself of his desire to stay connected to his wife. By practicing daily gratitude reminders, he strengthened his belief that he was lucky to be Noreen's husband. Larry never wanted to take his wife's affection for granted again. Nor would he ever allow his father to get be-tween him and Noreen again.

We have to resolve to stop our destructive behavior in order to truly become self-forgiving. Toni was determined to find a better-paying job. She made a long-term commitment to improve her family's financial well-being and to be able to support her chil-dren. Toni's positive intention was to take loving care of her chil-dren. Her long-term commitment included attending computer school regularly, cutting down on expenses, and taking classes in financial management.

Elaine's long-term commitment was to stay sober, develop good work habits, and be faithful to her husband. Her positive intention focused on doing a lot of personal growth in order to find greater happiness. Elaine attended twelve-step programs regularly, started counseling, and looked for a mentor who would help her develop good work habits. Elaine practiced the HEAL method regularly until she was no longer angry at her-self. She forgave herself and moved on successfully in her life and marriage.

These are some pretty strong examples of people who needed to forgive themselves. Perhaps in your own life the ways in which you need to be kinder to yourself are not so dramatic. Is your lover annoyed by a habit you can't or won't stop? Do you always leave the lights on when you go out, or forget to cancel the newspaper when you go on vacation? It is important to get in the habit of seeing your good points so that you can put your smaller failures in perspective. You need to be your own good friend so that you can cut yourself some slack.

The theme of this book is quite simple. You need to be as kind as possible to yourself and to your lover because you are both engaged in a very difficult task. Being in a relationship is incredibly demanding, and it asks more of us than we realize. Your odds of finding a satisfying relationship increase when you can be gentle, loving, and forgiving toward yourself and your partner. Remember that it is as important to be good to yourself as it is to be good to your lover. You are both important and need all the TLC you can get.

I created the following nine steps to self-forgiveness as a simple guide to being kind to yourself. These steps integrate the earlier lessons about forgiving your lover with the self-forgiveness techniques:

1. Be willing to feel your emotions about what you did. Try to articulate the specific wrong you have committed and the harm it caused. Tell a couple of trusted people about your experience.

2. Understand your goal. Forgiveness enables you to feel at peace about things you did that you wish you hadn't. You don't even have to reconcile with the person you have hurt to make peace with yourself.

3. Self-forgiveness can be defined as the recognition that we all make mistakes, that blame and shame can be replaced by making amends and developing better ways to behave, and that our grievance stories can be changed or even relinquished.

4. Recognize that your primary distress is coming from the hurt feelings, thoughts, and physical upset you are experiencing right now, not what you did two minutes ago or ten years ago. Make the commitment to yourself to feel better now.

5. Every time you feel upset over what you have done, practice PERT to soothe your body's fight-or-flight response.

6. Recognize your unenforceable rules that you be lovable and competent at all times. Remind yourself that every human being makes mistakes and has much to learn. Remind yourself that no one is a failure: each of us is only someone who was unable to successfully accomplish something at a particular place and time.

7. Learn to do good rather than feel bad. If you have hurt others or yourself, instead of mentally replaying the hurt, look for ways to apologize and make amends, and when necessary develop new skills so that you won't make the same mistake again.

8. Appreciate your good points. Take time out of each day to keep track of the kind and loving things you do.

9. Amend your grievance story to reflect your heroic choice to learn, grow, and forgive.

Self-forgiveness has much in common with forgiving your lover. Both involve taking someone's actions less personally, taking more personal responsibility for how you feel, and changing your grievance story to reflect your underlying positive intention. The impetus for both kinds of forgiveness is to heal yourself and your relationship and by doing so create the best life you can for yourself and your family. When you suffer less and focus on your positive intention, you offer the best you can to your marriage. That is because no one is perfect and everyone needs to be forgiven. We need to forgive the flaws of our lovers and of ourselves in order to live gently with them and ourselves. The scientific research suggests that we not only improve our mental and physical health as we do so but go a long way toward ensuring a successful and rewarding relationship and life.

TWELVE

Something to Keep in Mind

I want to take one last chance to remind you to take full advantage of the opportunity for growth and happiness you have with your intimate partner. Being loved is the greatest gift any of us will ever be given. We need to remain aware of the importance and fragility of this gift and to try to treat our partner with a gentle kindness. When you choose to forgive your lover and yourself, you honor that goal. Both the good news and the bad news about being in a relationship is that you will get many opportunities to practice forgiveness. With that in mind, I want to close this book by examining two simple ideas that put the finishing touch on forgiveness training for couples.

First, learning to forgive in your current relationship may be a good place to work on some of the wounds inflicted on you in your past by your parents or old lovers. Your painful past will matter less if you can succeed in your present relationship. In addition, much of what hurt us in the past resurfaces in the present with our lovers.

I have worked with so many people who were the product of troubled, nasty, or rejecting parents. I have heard countless stories of mistreatment and neglect. In forgiveness classes, people tell horror stories about lovers who abandoned them, were unfaithful, or failed to pay child support. Unfortunately, many of these people continue to struggle in conflicted, stressful, and unhappy relationships with their current partners. I encourage these people to put their focus on getting the current relationship right and obsessing less about the past.

I once counseled a man named Danny who was in his midthirties. Danny's parents had gone through a bitter divorce when he was young, and his home had been very dysfunctional. His mother was only marginally capable of parenting, and Danny spent much of his childhood without her guidance. His father was absent and did not contribute much to his care. Danny had a number of significant wounds from his parents that he could have benefited from forgiving. However, I told Danny to worry less about his parents' mistreatment and concentrate instead on making his relationship with his wife Yolanda work. I pointed out that working on his current relationship with his parents would make little difference in his life, but improving his relationship with Yolanda would vastly enhance his happiness.

As part of Danny's therapy, he had to forgive the difficult situations with Yolanda that were triggered by issues that first surfaced in his childhood. Danny chafed anytime he was told what to do, since he had mostly raised himself. He also suffered from poor problem-solving strategies, having received little adult guidance as a kid. Inevitably, Yolanda would tell Danny what to do or try to correct his poor planning and follow-through. Danny got mad every time one of these conversations happened. I told him to practice PERT on a regular basis and use his positive intention to have a loving relationship to motivate himself. He found, after much practice and struggle, that learning to create a successful relationship did wonders for his self-confidence and practicing forgiveness with someone he loved made it easier in more difficult situations.

What Danny connected with was the precious opportunity for a happy life that real love presents. He came into the relationship with Yolanda with a history of many relationship failures and the kind of issues from a troubled childhood that have crippled many other people's ability to create a satisfying relationship. When Danny committed himself to doing his best with Yolanda, he was forced to confront how much baggage he had brought to the relationship. He saw his anger and rebelliousness and had to decide how much of it to impose on his wife. He also saw how these habits allowed him to criticize and avoid Yolanda when she desperately wanted to connect with him. With forgiveness training, he was able to clearly see the loving and imperfect woman he was punishing for other people's offenses, and he chose to stop.

Rachel had been raised by loving parents, but damaged by a miserable first marriage. After the first few years of marriage, her husband started to neglect her and he ultimately cheated on her. He treated her as if she were stupid and could not be trusted. Since Rachel had always been loved and valued, she was unprepared for his bad treatment and stayed married longer than was good for her. She had been divorced for five years and dating Bruce for two when we first met. She really liked and respected Bruce, but her hesitancy and self-imposed roadblocks were ruining the relationship. Bruce loved her and wanted to marry her, but Rachel was scared and feared commitment.

I told Rachel that she had to forgive both her ex-husband and herself. The proof in the pudding of forgiveness would be her success in her current relationship with Bruce. Rachel first had to grieve the loss of innocence and safety she had experienced in her marriage. Then she had to forgive herself for both choosing her ex and staying married for too long. Then she needed to make amends to Bruce for bringing her failed marriage into their relationship. She did this by being extra kind and by forgiving his flaws, which she had exaggerated to keep him at a distance. In addition, Rachel was asked to create a HEAL statement that highlighted assertiveness as part of her long-term commitment. This was to make sure she did not let problems in the relationship fester, as had happened in her old, disastrous marriage.

The point is that when you want to focus on forgiveness, it is most important to do so in your current relationship. You do not want your marriage to be contaminated by past wounds. There will still be situations where your problems are clearly about someone other than your partner. There will be situations where you are lied to or mistreated and you simply have to deal with that other person. But take advantage of forgiveness. Be responsible for your negative behavior by making amends whenever possible, and practice being a better partner when you can.

The second simple idea that will help you finish up your forgiveness training is the reality that many long-term relationships require us to practice existential forgiveness as we struggle with issues that involve painful changes for which no specific person is to blame, such as aging bodies, children leaving home, and sickness. Life may present you with challenges that are not your fault and not your partner's fault. Difficult times may simply emerge as part of being alive. You and your partner will age, and if you live long enough, you will also decline physically and intellectually. These experiences call for existential forgiveness as you grieve and then make peace with a normal but painful part of life.

Existential forgiveness allows us to forgive the way life is even when it hurts. Sometimes life is simply difficult, and some transitions are simply painful. There are so many life experiences that can challenge us and require existential forgiveness. The birth of a child may put strain on a marriage. It may be painful when your children leave home. You may suffer when your parents die. Sometimes a job loss or an unavoidable natural disaster can test you. You and your partner will successfully come through all these kinds of situations by grieving and then letting go. Your relationship may have to weather storms that neither of you created. Even when the enemy is life itself, you can still dig inside and find the power to feel your pain, grieve your loss, be forgiving in your heart, and make the best of things. Along the way, you want to appreciate the lover you have. To whatever degree you can do this, you will have successfully applied one of the crucial secrets to a loving and lasting relationship.

Notes

———◆———

1. Issidoros Sarinopoulos, "Interpersonal Forgiveness and Physical Health," *The World of Forgiveness* 3 (2, 2000): 16–18.
2. Howard Tennen and Glenn Affleck, "Blaming Others for Threatening Events," *Psychological Bulletin* 108 (1990): 209–32.
3. K. A. Lawler, J. W. Younger, R. L. Piferi, E. Billington, R. Jobe, K. Edmondson, and W. H. Jones, "A Change of Heart: Cardiovascular Correlates of Forgiveness in Response to Interpersonal Conflict," *Journal of Behavioral Medicine* 26 (5, 2003): 373–93.
4. C. V. Witvliet, T. E. Ludwig, and K. L. Vander Laan, "Granting Forgiveness or Harboring Grudges: Implications for Emotion, Physiology, and Health," *Psychological Science* 12 (2001): 117–23.
5. D. Tibbits, D. Piromalli, F. M. Luskin, and G. Ellis, "Hypertension Reduction Through Forgiveness Training," *Journal of Pastoral Care and Counseling* 60 (Spring–Summer 2006): 27–34.
6. J. W. Carson, F. J. Keefe, V. Goli, A. M. Fras, T. R. Lynch, S. R. Thorp, and J. L. Buechler, "Forgiveness and Chronic Low Back Pain: A Preliminary Study Examining the Relationship of Forgiveness to Pain, Anger, and Psychological Distress," *Journal of Pain* 6 (2, 2005): 84–91.
7. Jon Webb, "Forgiveness and Health Promotion Among People with Spinal Cord Injury," paper presented at the Templeton Forgiveness Research Conference, Atlanta, GA (2004).
8. Loren Toussaint, "Forgiveness Is a Factor in Low Blood Pressure, Especially in Poorer Blacks," paper presented at the Templeton Forgiveness Research Conference, Atlanta, GA (2004).
9. A. H. Harris, F. M. Luskin, S. V. Benisovich, S. Standard, J. Bruning, S. Evans, and C. Thoresen, "Effects of a Group Forgiveness Intervention on Forgiveness, Perceived Stress, and Trait Anger: A Randomized Trial," *Journal of Clinical Psychology* 62 (6, 2006): 715–33.

10. Michael E. McCullough, Kenneth C. Rachal, Steven J. Sandage, Everett L. Worthington Jr., S. W. Brown, and T. L. Hight, "Interpersonal Forgiving in Close Relationships. II. Theoretical Elaboration and Measurement," *Journal of Personality and Social Psychology* 75 (1998): 1586–1603.

11. Amanda J. Rose and Steven R. Asher, "Children's Goals and Strategies in Response to Conflicts Within a Friendship," *Developmental Psychology* 35 (1999): 69–79.

12. John M. Gottman and Nan S. Silver, *The Seven Principles for Making Marriage Work* (New York: Crown/Three Rivers Press, 1999).

13. David L. Fenell, "Characteristics of Long-Term First Marriages," *Journal of Mental Health Counseling* 15 (1993): 446–60.

14. Jane R. Rosen-Grandon, Jane E. Myers, and John A. Hattie, "Marital Interaction Processes and Marital Satisfaction," *Journal of Counseling and Development* 82 (2004): 56–68.

15. Kristina Coop Gordon, "Demystifying Forgiveness: A Cognitive-Behavioral Stage Model of Forgiveness in Marital Relationships," *Dissertation Abstracts* (Chapel Hill: University of North Carolina, 1999).

16. Frank D. Fincham, Steven R. H. Beach, and Joanne Davila, "Forgiveness and Conflict Resolution in Marriage," *Journal of Family Psychology* 18 (2004): 72–81.

17. Dale Gene Battleson, "Forgiveness as a Factor in Marriage and in Conflict Resolution," *Dissertation Abstracts* (Lincoln: University of Nebraska, 1997).

18. Kristina Coop Gordon, Donald H. Baucom, and Douglas K. Snyder, "An Integrative Intervention for Promoting Recovery from Extramarital Affairs," *Journal of Marital and Family Therapy* 30 (2004): 213–31.

19. Julie H. Hall and Frank Fincham, "Relationship Dissolution Following Infidelity: The Roles of Attributions and Forgiveness," *Journal of Social and Clinical Psychology* 25 (5, 2006): 508–22.

20. Mark S. Rye, Kenneth I. Pargament, Wei Pan, David W. Yingling, Karrie A. Shogren, and Masako Ito, "Can Group Interventions Facilitate Forgiveness of an Ex-spouse? A Randomized Clinical Trial," *Journal of Consulting and Clinical Psychology* 73 (5, 2005): 880–92.

21. V. Stein, "The Importance of Forgiveness in Marital Therapy," *Dissertation Abstracts* (Miami: Carlos Albizu University, 2000).